ANOTHER GENERATION

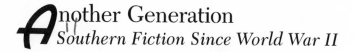

Another Generation
Southern Fiction Since World War II

LEWIS A. LAWSON

With a Foreword by
Thomas Daniel Young

UNIVERSITY PRESS OF MISSISSIPPI
Jackson

Library of Congress Cataloging in Publication Data

Lawson, Lewis A.
   Another generation.

   Includes index.
   1. American fiction—Southern States—History and
criticism.   2. Southern States in literature.
3. American fiction—20th century—History and
criticism.   I. Young, Thomas Daniel, 1919–
II. Title.
PS261.L38   1984   813'.54'09975   83-16738
ISBN 0-87805-196-1

One generation passeth away,
and another generation cometh:
but the earth abideth for ever.

ECCLESIASTES

CONTENTS

*L*ewis A. Lawson does not possess the critical reputation that his work merits because his perceptive and illuminating essays have appeared, for the most part, in journals of limited circulation. Although he has for years contributed to an impressive number of collections devoted to the works of an individual author, now for the first time the student or any other reader of contemporary southern letters will have readily available the helpful commentary of, to alter slightly John Crowe Ransom's comment on Cleanth Brooks, "the best reader of difficult . . . [contemporary fiction] alive."

In a thoroughly researched and convincingly argued essay Lawson contends that between 1920 and 1950 the South experienced a literary renascence that can be compared with the literary flowering of New England a hundred years earlier, but, he insists, the Southern Renaissance did not end in 1950: "The prevailing mode of its fiction may have changed it is true; the generation of the twenties had to fight to be realistic while the present generation feels compelled to be extra-realistic." Allen Tate characterizes the literature of his age—that of Faulkner, Ransom, Tate, Warren, and Wolfe—in a slightly different manner. "With the War of 1914–1918," he wrote in 'The New Provincialism,' "the South reentered the world—but gave a backward glance as it stepped over the border; that backward glance gave us the Southern renascence, a literature conscious of the past in the present." Lewis Simpson wrote that the important Southern writers between World War I and World War II "inaugurated a struggle to comprehend the nature of memory and history"; they were specifically interested in attempting to demonstrate the "redemptive meaning of the classical-Christian past in its bearing on the present." After World War II, he continues, the significant Southern writers concluded that "any attempt to establish a new literary covenant is futile." These writers were convinced that their only subject was to attempt to demonstrate the existence of some acceptable relationship between themselves and an apparently absurd universe. To make their separate existence plausible and significant in a universe from which the gods have disappeared, these contemporary writers—those whose best work began to appear after World War II—felt compelled to resort to techniques that would make their work appear "extra-real." It is to this latter generation of writers that Lawson devotes most of his attention.

To demonstrate what he means by "extra-realistic" Lawson presents examples of two different fictional techniques: the grotesque and the existential/phenomenological. Flannery O'Connor's *Wise Blood* (1952), Lawson writes, is a classic example of the grotesque. It is a "novel only in the widest possible sense of the word. It is a prose fiction of considerable length, but beyond that requirement none of the standard elements of the novel is to be found. The development of character, the exploration of character interaction, and the development of plot are unimportant. Such action as occurs is often without motivation, leads nowhere, and is most always absurd. Any resemblance to the world of objective reality is certainly incidental." After this disclaimer, Lawson allows us to follow his careful and exhaustive reading of the novel so that we are thoroughly convinced that through the use of no other technique could O'Connor have accomplished her objective so completely. As O'Connor stated many times the intention of her fiction was to depict the reality of Christianity to an audience for whom nothing transempirical is real. "She was uninterested," Lawson concludes, "in the felicities of the art of conventional fiction, and felt completely free to use absurdity, paradox, and illogicality, if those were the only media which could carry her vision."

Most of the other essays in this collection rely upon critics of the existential/phenomenological persuasion to assess the artistic intention and execution of the contemporary Southern writer. One of the most helpful of the essays is on Richard Wright's *The Outsider* (1953). Many critics see Wright's career as anticlimactic after *Native Son* (1940) and *Black Boy* (1945), but obviously Lawson does not agree. If *The Outsider* is read in the light of Kierkegaard's *The Concept of Dread*, it is obvious that Wright is offering a Christian, and not an atheistic, existential view, and this book, as well as Wright's earlier ones, is essential if we are to know the quality of the Black experience in the twentieth century.

In "The Knife and the Saw in *The Dollmaker*," Lawson uses Martin Heidegger's *Being and Time* to reveal the meaning of Harriette Arnow's novel. From the opening scene it is obvious that Gertie Nevels, Arnow's heroine, has avoided the subject/object split that has caused so much alienation for modern man. She not only has a very strong sense of place, of someone living somewhere, she has absolute confidence in her ability to protect her home. She has not the scientific view of reality discussed by Jean Paul Sartre in *Being and Nothingness;* she does not think of a thing as "stripped of all instrumentality." She considers a thing fundamentally as it relates to her as a tool, an instrument, a vessel and secondarily, if at all, as a composition of properties and characteristics. Because she considers the knife she holds merely as an extension of her hand, she is able to use it to perform a tracheotomy on her ill son Amos and cut a poplar switch for a pipe to insert in the incision so her son can breathe. Because she imposes her existence on her environment, she is able to force the military general, who represents only abstract, mechanical power, to take her son to the hospital.

Through a series of moves Gertie finally ends up in the city where she is just one drop in an ocean of undifferentiated humanity. Here saws are used to turn out millions of identical articles instead of the individually handicrafted dolls she had whittled back home. War and strikes bring hard times, and Clovis, Gertie's husband, uses her knife to kill the man who has injured him. Finally, in a scene replete with Biblical allusions, Gertie is presented as a majestic woman, willing to sacrifice herself for the future of her children, but her ultimate action proclaims that she is willing to submit to nothing but herself.

Lawson's study of Cass Kinsolving, the protagonist of William Styron's *Set This House on Fire* (1960), is based on Kierkegaardian philosophy. The young American artist is sick, suffering from "despair and self-loathing." He is, he says on another occasion "sick unto death," and the only plausible explanation, Lawson suggests, is that Cass is traveling "through the stages of despair until he reaches the faith that saves him from madness." In short, Lawson posits, only the modern *malaise*, which Kierkegaard presents in *The Sickness Unto Death*, can provide a reasonable motivation for Cass's actions and a consistent pattern for his development as a character. Then in a manner typical of his critical method, Lawson carefully goes through the major episodes of the novel and collects the evidence to support his thesis. (The argument in the essay on Mitchell F. Jayne's *Old Fish Hawk*—"*Old Fish Hawk:* From Stereotype to Archetype"— is developed in basically the same manner, although here the theme is different. Rather than developing his thesis around some element of existential/phenomenological philosophy, Lawson demonstrates how the essential action of the novel is developed around the stereotypical statement "that men of the dark castes have a valuable wisdom to offer the sons of the white caste." He supports his argument with references to novelists— James Fenimore Cooper, Mark Twain, Joel Chandler Harris, William Faulkner, and other American writers.)

Lawson's most enduring critical writing, I suspect, is included in the various essays he has written on the fiction of Walker Percy. Of all the commentators on Percy's fictional creations, he is, I believe, the one most thoroughly convinced of the influence of Percy's Southern background upon his art. The essay in this collection that most adequately represents the convictions I have in mind is "William Alexander Percy, Walker Percy, and the Apocalypse." In this piece Lawson utilizes the history of the Percy family, William Alexander Percy's poem, "Enzio's Kingdom" (1924), and his autobiography, *Lanterns on the Levee*

(1941), The career of Frederick II of Sicily (1194–1250), the theological speculations of Joachim, a twelfth-century abbot, and the *Meditations* of Marcus Aurelius to provide a basis for a consistent interpretation of Walker Percy's first four novels: *The Moviegoer* (1961), *The Last Gentleman* (1966), *Love in the Ruins* (1971), and *Lancelot* (1977).

In the other Percy essay in the collection Lawson again goes to the work of Jean Paul Sartre and other existentialist philosophers to show how moviegoing functions as theme in *The Moviegoer.* Binx Bolling's vertical search, his attempt to find his relationship to the universe by reading "essential books" was not completely satisfying because "though the universe is disposed of, I myself was left out." This debilitating conclusion was reached because Bolling had discovered Sartre's conviction of the inability of the scientific method to consider a "thing in its thingness"; it views a thing as "stripped of all instrumentality." Because instrumentality is left out, man is left out, for to man the essential quality of a thing is how it relates to him as a tool, an instrument, a utensil. Thus after Binx has read all the "fundamental" books, he finds himself, as Sartre says, "de trop" or superfluous.

In this condition he enters Sartre's state of "fascination," or, as Binx expresses it, "wonder." Now, he says, "I wander seriously and sit and read as a diversion." Binx becomes, he feels, an exile in a "desert world," a "world without men." He organizes his life around emptiness. He reads *Arabia Deserta* behind the covers of a Standard and Poor binder as he practices his daytime profession as a stockbroker, although he always "conceives of himself as a ghost wandering a deserted space." At night he goes to movies, always talking to the owner or ticket seller because if he did not he feels he might be "lost, cut loose metaphysically speaking." He would be seeing "one copy of a film which might be shown anywhere at any time. There is a danger of slipping clean out of space and time." The movie itself presents "patterns of behavior he might emulate," Lawson argues, and thereby escape the modern *malaise,* the "sickness unto death." The movies also provide means of preventing the modern affliction of everydayness, the feeling of being anyone living anywhere, by presenting examples of "certification," "repetition," and "rotation"—terms that Percy discusses in *The Message in the Bottle* (1975).

In few other places can one find so clearly, effectively, and convincingly stated, the fundamental differences between *modern* and *contemporary* fiction—why the "present generation feels compelled to be extra-realistic," the means by which contemporary writers apprehend reality, and the artistic manner in which they reconstitute it—than in the present collection of essays.

THOMAS DANIEL YOUNG
Vanderbilt University

PREFACE

I was born in Bristol, which is divided by a line into Tennessee and Virginia. I was born on the Tennessee side and was for many years vain of that fact. Not that I minded visiting on the Virginia side; but I never stayed all night over there. The boys in my neighborhood thought it very funny that the Virginia side had the depot and all three hotels (two respectable enough to be on postcards) and yet was not a real place. While the Tennessee side was comforting, somehow. In the spring, when I attended the tent revival, I could understand the preacher when he dwelled upon man's disobedience and expulsion from Eden: Adam and Eve were sent to live on the Virginia side.

I learned early about living on the line. I guess that I discovered the awful truth by the age of six, that every day innocent people just like me were taken across the line to live. It was, come to think of it, actually strange that we lived on the Tennessee side. For my father worked at the tannery, over on the Virginia side, and it took him at least ten minutes to drive home at noon. It would have made much more sense for us to live over there. At the time that I discovered this split world, we were renting and could just as well have rented over there. I must have thought that nobody else in the family had figured this out, and I certainly was not going to tell. But that willful silence probably led to my psychology of living on the line. I was always scared that somebody else would figure it out, and one day I'd come home from school and see the curtain stretchers tied to the top of the car; I was also guilt ridden, knowing that I ought to reveal the secret that would have helped the family and cost me only my feeling of being at home. Both emotions worked on my self, for I was becoming both anxious about being in any new place and guilty about being where I was. By junior high, I was growing self the way other boys were growing facial hair.

In short, I was becoming fit for nothing but literature, which seems often to be about life split by the line. It never occurred to me to write it, but I did decide, after a while, to teach it. For graduate school, I went far across the line, to Madison, Wisconsin, filled with high hopes, but no particular plan. By the end of the first afternoon, I had decided to specialize in Southern literature. I see now the reason for such a conversion: I had been in danger of getting too far from the line. When I finished my graduate work, I got a job at the University of Maryland. At the time my choice of a school did not seem significant: I simply preferred it to my other possibilities, one in Minnesota and the other in Texas. It was several years before I noticed that Maryland was called "the Old Line State."

Northerners tell me that the thing that they like (or do not like) about Maryland is that it is southern. Northern, say the southerners. I disagree with both, for it seems like no place at all, to me. But I have found that a place that seems like no place is the only place for me. If I lived any farther North, it would be tempting to teach an abstraction, *Southern Literature,* instead of a novel written by a southerner. If I lived any farther South, it might be too easy to teach a novel as a proof text for southern history or sociology. As it is, being betwixt and between, myself, I remember to point out the ways that a novel is both of the South and yet not altogether.

I have tried to do the same thing in my essays, which mostly have to do with the southern novel since 1945, a period when southern writers have been torn between their response to the continuing southern presence and their awareness that a southerner must now be depicted as having pretty much the same range of emotions as anyone else. I think that I am a very old-fashioned writer on literature: for the most part I offer a "reading" of a novel, usually some novel that I teach or plan to teach.

The "reading" is usually an attempt to uncover, not southern, but somewhat more universal, themes, concerns, behavior. The generalization that I use may be from one of several disciplines, whatever seems to fit the particular novel, just as long as it helps to draw the line in the novel between here and elsewhere. Flannery O'Connor once said, to quote her very loosely, that for her a novel was a life-and-death matter. To judge from the novels that I have written about here, I must agree, for they all head in that direction.

I wish to express my gratitude to the following journals for permission to reprint material appearing in this book:

Texas Quarterly, for "Twentieth-Century Southern Fiction: 'One generation passeth away, and another generation cometh . . .,'" originally entitled "Portrait of a Culture in Crisis: Modern Southern Literature."

Renascence, for "*Wise Blood* and the Grotesque," originally entitled "Flannery O'Connor and the Grotesque: *Wise Blood.*"

CLA Journal, for "Cross Damon: Kierkegaardian Man of Dread."

Appalachian Heritage, for "The Knife and the Saw in *The Dollmaker.*"

Wisconsin Studies in Contemporary Literature, for "Cass Kinsolving: Kierkegaardian Man of Despair."

Southern Quarterly, for "Moviegoing in *The Moviegoer.*"

American Indian Quarterly, for "*Old Fish Hawk:* From Stereotype to Archetype."

Modern Age, for "William Alexander Percy, Walker Percy, and the Apocalypse."

I am happy to acknowledge support:

To the General Education Board, for a grant which enabled me to venture across the line to Wisconsin.

To the General Research Board of the University of Maryland, for several Summer Research Awards and for a Book Subsidy Award.

To Miss Betty B. Baehr, Interlibrary Loan Librarian, McKel-
din Library, University of Maryland, who has never failed to
make sense of my confused requests.

I dedicate my work here to Barbara—when it was time to seek
a wife, I went over on the Virginia side.

LEWIS A. LAWSON
June 1983

ANOTHER GENERATION

Twentieth-Century Southern Fiction

"One generation passeth away,
and another generation cometh . . ."

*I*n 1917 the irreverent Mr. Mencken of Baltimore, in "The Sahara of the Bozart," drafted an obituary of the South. "It would be impossible," he wrote, "in all history to match so complete a drying-up of a civilization." Especially notorious, in Mr. Mencken's eyes, was the state of southern literature. He prefaced his essay with a quotation from "the lamented J. Gordon Coogler": "Alas, for the South! Her books have grown fewer—She never was much given to literature." Only one contemporary southern writer escaped Mr. Mencken's contempt: "Once you have counted James Branch Cabell (a lingering survivor of the *ancien régime:* a scarlet dragon-fly imbedded in opaque amber) you will not find a single southern prose writer, who can actually write."

Perhaps there were no others who could meet his dicta, although his failure to recognize Ellen Glasgow must certainly be questioned. There were, however, several authors, who, if they could not write, could very easily be read. These writers were the manufacturers of the southern myth. For the most part the fiction of these authors contained romantic idealizations of southern military gallantry and feminine fortitude, or melodramatic depictions of aristocratic endurance during abolitionist provocation before the War, Yankee invasion, and finally Carpetbag-Negro-Scalawag Reconstruction. Hostilities were hardly over when the glorification of the defeated armies commenced; John Esten Cooke wrote *Surry of Eagle's Nest* in 1866, and the next year Sidney Lanier, *Tiger-Lilies.* Thereafter, novels presenting the southern cause from the southern point of view were constantly being published. By 1917 southern war novels had been written by, among others, Thomas Nelson Page, F. Hopkinson Smith, George Washington Cable, James Lane Allen, Winston Churchill, Mary Johnston, Ellen Glasgow, Thomas Dixon, George Cary Eggleston, and John Fox, Jr.

All of this is to say that Mencken was very much wrong. He may not have approved of the southern civilization, culture, or literature that he observed, but they had effectively satisfied southern needs for fifty years. In thousands of towns and villages much of southern civil life revolved around the statue of the Confederate soldier, eyes vigilant under his kepi or slouch hat, still facing north, like the one that dominates the last scene of Faulkner's *The Sound and the Fury.* Confederate veterans dominated southern politics from the end of Reconstruction until the First World War. Since the Protestant South viewed Christmas and Easter as Popish celebrations, Thanksgiving as a New England luxury, and the Fourth of July as a Negro holiday, the most solemn ritual was Confederate Monument Day or Confederate Memorial Day, when, one observer notes, "the whole population of a town turns out in procession, headed by the Ladies Memorial Association, and decorates the graves." Especially was the myth fostered by such publications as *The Land We Love* (1860–1869), *The Southern Bivouac* (1882–1887), and *The Confederate Veteran*, representing the United Confederate Veterans, the United Daughters of the Confederacy, the Sons of Confederate Veterans, the Confederated Southern Memorial Association, and other such groups, which endured through forty volumes until 1932.

What is suggested by all the devotion to the Lost Cause and the deference to its veterans is that the South prior to the First World War was, in relation to the remainder of the United States, a tradition-directed society, in the terminology of David Riesman's *The Lonely Crowd.* It had a high growth potential, both in terms of population and of production. It had a high degree of conformity dictated by family, caste, and historical circumstance. It received few of the immigrants who were pouring into the other areas of the United States. It was a Solid South—united, much more so than during the War itself, by devotion to a Confederate past, the Democratic Party, the Protestant Church, and a fierce antipathy toward the freed Negro. It depended upon myth, legend, and song for most of its cultural coherence, upon a literature of moonlight and magnolias for the remainder.[1]

Yet there had been some vocal discontent with the domination of the southern myth ever since the 1880s. And this discontent became increasingly aggressive as southern cultural patterns became more rigid in the last years of the century because of the failure of the Populistic impulse and of the introduction of segregation and Negro disfranchisement. In a sense certain Confederates were responsible for the growing disenchantment with the myth. Defeated by the Yankees, they seemed determined to champion the myth but to practice the opposite; many Confederate Brigadiers became Southern Bourbons, those Southerners of upper class who aligned themselves with Northern capitalists intent upon exploiting the South. Many became involved in questionable activities, in railroad manipulation, land grants, and speculation, and others lent their names to notorious schemes.

So it was that there were many young people in the South who could accept Mencken's assertions about their homeland. The first response came from New Orleans. In January 1921, a protege of Mencken, John McClure, along with Julius Weis Friend and Basil Thompson, offered the first monthly issue of *The Double Dealer.* It early made its editorial position clear; the June 1921, issue contained a pronouncement on "Southern Letters":

> It is high time, we believe, for some doughty, clear visioned penman to emerge from the sodden marshes of Southern literature. We are sick to death of the treacly sentiments with which our well-intentioned lady fictioneers regale us. The old traditions are no more. New peoples, customs prevail. The Confederacy has long since been dissolved. A storied realm of dreams, lassitude, pleasure,

chivalry and the Nigger no longer exists. We have our Main Streets
here, as elsewhere.

The Double Dealer is now most famous for the first publication
of the prose of William Faulkner, in 1925, but his pieces for it
were inconsequential, and a much more solid claim to its
significance lies in its sponsorship of dozens of young writers,
including Hamilton Basso, Donald Davidson, John Crowe Ransom, Allen Tate, and Robert Penn Warren.

In another quarter, Richmond, late capital of the Confeder-
acy, *The Reviewer* began publication in February 1921. *Preju-
dices: Second Series* was on the counter by then, and Hunter
Stagg reviewed it in the first issue of the Richmond publication.
Stagg admitted the truth of Mencken's charges, and Mencken
delightedly offered to help the editors establish their enterprise.
As a result of the aid of Mencken and others, including James
Branch Cabell, Carl Van Vechten, Joseph Hergesheimer, and
Alfred A. Knopf, *The Reviewer* frequently had the best issue of
any little magazine in the United States, featuring such southern
authors as Mary Johnston, Ellen Glasgow, Frances Newman,
and Julia Peterkin.

Still another little magazine began publication in April 1922,
in Nashville. This was *The Fugitive*, destined to become, because of the lasting coherence and growing fame of its sponsors,
better remembered than its predecessors *The Double Dealer*
and *The Reviewer.* Among the names associated with this journal
are Sidney Mttron Hirsch, John Crowe Ransom, Merrill Moore,
Allen Tate, Donald Davidson, and Robert Penn Warren. In its
first issue was an unsigned editorial by John Crowe Ransom that
identified its kinship with the new attitude of young southern
writers:

> Official exception having been taken by the sovereign people to the
> mint julep, a literary phase known rather euphemistically as South-
> ern Literature has expired, like any other stream whose source is
> stopped up. The demise was not untimely: among other advantages
> THE FUGITIVE is enabled to come to birth in Nashville, Tennessee
> under a star not entirely unsympathetic. THE FUGITIVE flees from

nothing faster than from the high-caste Brahmins of the Old South. . . .

Such jaunty iconoclasm suggests the influence of Mencken, and indeed a copy was sent for his approval. His comment was appropriately Delphian; he designated *The Fugitive* "at the moment, the entire literature of Tennessee."

Thus did the Southern Renaissance begin. It seemed to develop spontaneously all over the South, with each contributing group separated from and not particularly aware of the plans of the other groups. If there does appear to be a general unity of outlook and intention, it is perhaps because many of the leading spirits, like Ransom, Davidson, and Faulkner, were veterans of the First World War, and they came back, as veterans always have, with a fresh perspective on their own country. It should be noted that none of these groups planned a defense of the South or an attack upon the North; their editorials suggest that they only wanted to look clearly at their homeland.

It is frequently suggested that the Fugitives best typify the first decade of the renascence, and it is tempting to make such a suggestion, since their poetry, fairly similar in quality and in type, implies a unified trend, even a new school of southern thought. What must be remembered, however, is that the Nashville Fugitives represented only a very small number of writers, whose social concerns at the time were not notably pronounced. Aesthetically the Fugitives may represent the best southern writing of the twenties; it is, however, the work of many new southern novelists which offers the most accurate picture of the state of southern thought and society during that decade.[2]

The most striking characteristic of southern fiction in the twenties is its diversity of subject matter.[3] There is no radical change, it is true, in the work of James Branch Cabell and Ellen Glasgow, the established southern writers. But younger southern writers vividly emphasized the growing disjunction that was occurring in the southern imagination. Even in that favorite southern staple, the Civil War novel, there was a greater degree of realism and a greater amount of objectivity.[4] The healthy increase of realism is also apparent in novels dealing with the mountainous regions of the South.[5] Indications of a changing outlook are even more marked in novels dealing with the crisis in the social order.[6] But perhaps most indicative of the intention of the younger southern writers to look without blinders at their own society is the new portrayal of the Negro in their fiction.[7]

The year 1929 must be accounted the climax of the first phase of the Southern Renaissance, indeed one of the most significant years in all southern literary history. Ellen Glasgow contributed one of her best studies of changing Virginia manners as she presented compromised women of three different generations in *They Stooped to Folly.* DuBose Heyward followed up his success with Porgy by presenting a warm portrait of an old Negro blessed with terrific endurance, in *Mamba's Daughters.* Stark Young revealed the discrepancy of attitude between traditional southerner and new southerner, in *River House.* And Cabell's *The Way of Ecben* continued his exploration of Poictesme.

There was also a persistence of good fiction in areas explored earlier in the decade. Fiswoode Tarleton's *Bloody Ground* received excellent reviews for its depiction of a southern mountain community. Evelyn Scott's *The Wave* presented the Civil War in more density and complexity than any previous novel. In *School Girl,* Carmen Barnes followed those who had hinted that Lilith could be found below the Mason-Dixon Line, and in *Cora Potts,* Ward Greene offered a lively justification for a poor white girl's success through the only profession in which she excelled. Robert Emmet Kennedy gave another sensitive treatment of the Negro quarter of a small southern town, in *Red Bean Row,* while Dorothy Scarborough's *Can't Get a Redbird* again analyzed the punishing life of the sharecropper.

Had none of these novels been written, the year 1929 would still have been an *annus mirabilis* for southern fiction, though, for it ushered in four writers, who among them were to explored the ranges of the southern reality and bring it to the attention of the entire country. With *The Bastard,* Erkine Caldwell began his study of the elemental and grotesque in the lower class southerner. Prolific nearly beyond belief, Caldwell is best known for his *God's Little Acre* (1933), which sold over five million copies in a paperback edition between 1946 and 1950. Also in 1929 one of the *Double Dealer* group, Hamilton Basso, wrote his first novel, *Relics and Angels,* which reveals the ineffectiveness of southern training in preparing its young men to cope with reality. This novel does not, however, reveal the qualities—displayed in *A View from Pompey's Head* (1954) and *The Light Infantry Ball* (1959)—that make Basso one of the most popular southern novelists. The most remarkable first novel of the year was Thomas Wolfe's *Look Homeward, Angel.* Its strength lies, paradoxically, in both its synthesis of segments of southern fiction already fashionable and its freshness and narrowness of observation. It is concerned with an artist in the bud, just as Cabell or even Poe had written spiritual autobiography. It has a setting in the southern hills, is sympathetic toward the poorer southerner, and ridicules the established southern code. Yet at the same time it is life really not of the without, but of the within, for it is life only as it could be experienced by Eugene Gant. But beyond all of these qualities, it is the language of *Look Homeward, Angel,* the impression received that words are loved in their own right, that raises this novel above the earlier novels of the renascence.

But even yet the culmination of the year had not been reached. Before 1929 William Faulkner had given no hint that he was to make his name synonymous with southern fiction. His first two novels were very much derivative of the times; *Soldiers' Pay* (1926) dealt with the homecoming of a horribly wounded war veteran, and *Mosquitoes* (1927) was an attempt to satirize New Orleans literary types. His third published novel, *Sartoris,* suggested that he might become a southern novelist; as he later said: "Beginning with *Sartoris* I discovered that my own little postage stamp of native soil was worth writing about and that I would never live long enough to exhaust it, and that by sublimating the actual into the apocryphal I would have complete liberty to use whatever talent I might have to its absolute top."

It is in *The Sound and the Fury* (also 1929), however, that Faulkner exhibited his genius so completely that all successive southern writers have been automatically compared with him. Perhaps its strongest initial interest resides in its justly famed experimental techniques, especially the dislocation of sequential time and the rendering of the consciousness of the idiot Benjy. Judged purely as a southern novel, though, it should be viewed as nearly exhaustive orchestration of themes and subjects inherent in the genre: the fragmentation of the southern world view; the compulsive brooding upon defeat; the decline of the patricians into genteel impotence, drunkenness, neurotic invalidism, sexual promiscuity, idiocy, and materialism; the introduction of the purely grasping view of life later embodied in the Snopes clan; and the salutation to a race apparently better equipped than its ostensible superiors to mark the time and sort out the pieces of reality. Because of these and other qualities, *The Sound and the Fury* remains *the* southern novel for most people.

With so much literary activity in Mencken's "Sahara," it was inevitable that critics would begin to make some generalizations about the results. Herschel Brickell in 1927, in an article in the *Bookman* entitled "The Literary Awakening in the South," was one of the first to call attention to the freshness and variety of the new fiction. A little later Eudora Richardson, also in the *Bookman*, praised the new fiction for retaining the stress upon the indigenous that was customarily found in southern writing, while casting it in a realistic mode previously unassociated with that body of literature.

These articles suggest the larger issue that was beginning to be explored in the late twenties: the viability of traditional southern ways of looking at the world. The extremes of this issue were expressed in articles appearing in 1929. First the novelist Maristan Chapman (actually a husband-and-wife team, John S. H. Chapman and Mary Hamilton Chapman) proposed, in the *Century* that only through the retention of its conservative, tra-

ditional, agrarian philosophy could the South maintain its individuality. Then, in an apparent reply, Mencken's *American
Mercury* published W. J. Cash's "The Mind of the South,"[8]
which argued that the South deserved individuality only if it
threw off its reliance upon Southern Shintoism, superstition,
hypocrisy, and Confederate cant.

With such articles as these began what Mencken gleefully
called the "uprising in the Confederacy." It is frequently forgotten that there were two opposing points of view within southern
thought itself, so completely did one group—the Agrarians—
capture the imagination of both North and South. The battle was
not joined over whether or not the South should become a
province of the North; it had, in fact, been in that unhappy
circumstance for sixty-five years. On the contrary, differences of
opinion lay in the charting of a course by which the South could
recapture its individuality.

On the one hand were the social scientists, primarily, who
argued that economic progress was necessary for independence.
Representative of this group was Howard W. Odum, of the University of North Carolina, who, in his *An American Epoch*
(1930), wrote of "Uncle John," who possessed all the virtues
praised by southern spokesmen, who had fought in the rain
right up to Appomattox, but who now wanted only "to forget":
"Work, that was the thing. He was afraid the South was not
willing to pay the price of hard work, necessary to win its victory." If it would pay the price, Odum envisioned, like Henry
Grady before him, a new South.

The opponents of Odum's view were the Nashville Fugitive-
Agrarians, who chose not to "forget," but to remember. Also in
1930, twelve of them, finding that they were of similar mind
about many areas of their experience, decided to furnish their
views upon the best future course for the South. Each contributed an essay to a collection, which was entitled *I'll Take My
Stand* (Harper). Although the essayists were of similar mind,
they were not of identical mind; it is risky, therefore, to generalize about the message by citing two or three texts from different

sections of the book. There is, however, an "Introduction: A Statement of Principles," which states the degree to which all the essays are of a piece: "all tend to support a southern way of life against what may be called the American or prevailing way; and all as much as agree that the best terms in which to represent the distinction are contained in the phrase, Agrarian *versus* Industrial."

It was unfortunate that the group chose to use "agrarianism" as a rally cry. At a time when many southern farmers were hungry, "agrarianism" raised for most southerners a realistic picture of hard, unrewarding work, not an ideal program of Jeffersonian principles. But, as Louis D. Rubin, Jr. has very perceptively pointed out, the best known and most persuasive of the essayists—John Crowe Ransom, Donald Davidson, Allen Tate, Robert Penn Warren, Stark Young, Andrew Lytle, and John Gould Fletcher—were poets, not farmers, and they thought like poets; "they were given to the image." Rubin's description of the book and its function is apt: "this book of essays, and the vision of an agrarian South depicted in it, can best be considered as an extended metaphor, of which the image of the agrarian community is the figure, standing for and embodying something else. The something else is modern society."

Even the most casual trip into the South today will reveal that the warnings of the Agrarians were not heeded. Failure to provide a course of practical action does not denigrate, however, the significance of *I'll Take My Stand.* Its contributors were completely successful in articulating the primary myth that was to support southern fiction for a generation. Badly stated, this myth contains two opposing clusters of images. One cluster pictures a chaotic, frenzied, acquisitive life fruitlessly performed by impotent automatons. The opposing cluster contains a conception of rural or semi-rural life enriched by tradition, religion, stable and predictable social behavior, and feelings of individual worth.

The configurations of these two clusters were early sketched by Faulkner. *Sanctuary* (1931) describes the threat, Popeye

Vitelli, the machine-made man. In later works, particularly *The Hamlet* (1940), Faulkner identified other elements contributing to cultural upheaval, as he discovered the Snopeses, those vermin motivated only by greed, who, as it turned out, had been tunneling under the southern social structure ever since the outbreak of the War. The opposing cluster, the meaningful life, had first appeared when young Bayard Sartoris had visited the rural MacCallum clan in *Sartoris* (1929). It, too, was extensively amplified as Faulkner continued his saga. *The Hamlet* suggests the rural Frenchman's Bend as a kind of latter-day Eden, and "The Bear," in the cycle of stories *Go Down, Moses* (1942) depicts the possibility of moral transformation for anyone humble enough to learn from the forest and its priesthood, the hunters and the primitives.

Despite Faulkner's imposing achievement during the thirties, the success of other southern novelists should not be ignored. There was at least a score of these craftsmen,[9] and their efforts enabled the South to capture a remarkable number of literary awards. T. S. Stribling, Caroline Miller, Margaret Mitchell, and Marjorie Kinnan Rawlings claimed Pulitzer Prizes during the decade, and southern novels virtually dominated the best seller lists. Margaret Mitchell's *Gone with the Wind* (1936) proved to be the publishing event of the decade, as it so completely captured the imagination of the country that Macmillan Company answered orders for 50,000 copies on one day alone. One million copies were sold in six months, and before the novel lost its hold on the public, 3,500,000 copies were sold.

Besides the popular novelists, there were those who were to take their place as southern novelists of critical acclaim. With *Penhally* (1931), Caroline Gordon began a series of novels that have gained for her a reputation as a "writer's writer." So sustained is the quality of her work that enthusiasm for it is more and more evident. Katherine Anne Porter also began her career during this period. Although her best is in a relatively unpopular field, the novella, Miss Porter's work is of such consistently high quality that it is perhaps the most frequently used standard by

which the efforts of new southern writers may be judged. One of
the Fugitive novelists, Andrew Lytle, must be accounted among
the best southern novelists of the thirties. Although his work has
been considered uneven by some critics, his willingness to inno-
vate, to risk doing well in order that he might do better, assures
him a place among the craftsmen of the southern group. Another
Fugitive who turned to fiction is Robert Penn Warren, whose
work has enjoyed both critical and popular success. The settings
of his novels range the South both in space and in time, revealing a mind acutely responsive to the perplexing nature of history.

By the late thirties there was a general awareness that southern fiction constituted certainly the most coherent, and possibly
the most significant, movement in contemporary American literature. As a result, more and more critical attention was focussed
upon the qualities that motivated and enriched the work of these
writers. It was a happy coincidence that many southern writers
were exceptions to the old quip that the South was a place where
everybody could write and nobody could read; many southern
writers were excellent readers, and their criticism of modern
southern literature became widely noted for its informative,
even brilliant, quality, and the journals in which it appeared—
the *Southern Review*, the *Sewanee Review*, the *Kenyon Review*,
and the *Virginia Quarterly Review*—were among the most influential in the United States.

Through the efforts of academic critics and such writer-critics
as Donald Davidson, Caroline Gordon, Allen Tate, Andrew Lytle, and Robert Penn Warren, the origins and outlines of modern
southern literature were thoroughly explored. Critics had long
stressed the relationship between Edgar Allan Poe and modern
southern fiction, but beyond this association it was fashionable
to assert that the modern group was sustained by no indigenous
tradition. More and more, however, critics began to glimpse a
rough, realistic, even grotesque, tradition of violence, humor,
and the vernacular that had always existed as the antithesis to
the moonlight-and-magnolia school. They discovered the in-

fluence and pervasive popularity of the Old Southwest Humorists, such men as A. B. Longstreet, Johnson J. Hooper, Joseph G. Baldwin, and George W. Harris, who flourished during the generation before the War. And, too, as they began to discount the animosity that earlier southern critics had held toward George Washington Cable because of his social views, they saw that in Cable the postwar South had possessed a realism ranking with Mark Twain and William Dean Howells.

By this time, also, the basic outlines of modern southern fiction were traced, as critics began to investigate the southerner's conception of his relations with himself, with other people, and with his idea of the transcendent. In southern fiction the critics discovered that the southerner considered himself first of all a free moral agent. His actions were not determined by forces, either exterior or interior, of which he was unaware and over which he had no control; most southerners simply did not respond to the various forms of either social or psychological determinism. The southerner felt himself responsible for his actions, and for the actions of his ancestors. As a result of past evils and present failings, most southerners suffered from guilt and were driven to violent and extreme ways either to deny or to expiate it. But the southerner did not suffer from the nameless anxiety concomitant with urban, industrialized existence, the anxiety that drained off all vitality and love of life, the anxiety that compelled people to live frantically, yet fruitlessly. Consequently, the southerner, like the Puritan, could appear to relish his existence—when he was not beset by his sense of guilt.

It also became apparent that a good part of southern fiction was a catalogue of disintegration. Although their attitude toward the process of disintegration might vary, most southern authors realized that the once emphatic sense of family, social, and religious integrity was disappearing. Such a mood of disintegration cultivated a prevailing sense of both personal and regional defeat. The southerner thus had a sense of the tragic, for he, unlike any other American, could articulate and even accept personal defeat, since he looked upon man as a limited creature in the first place and since he could use the historical analogue of the prototypical defeat suffered in the War that was available to him. Critics, as a result, began to see that much of the historical matter of southern fiction was neither retrogressive escapism nor chauvinism, but rather a readily available method of apprehending the present. The past existed not merely for its own sake, but because it provided the metaphors through which the present could be described and understood. Shared history could provide ready reference points for private experience. And having realized that the southern past was really "mythic"—but not "mythic" in the sense of glossing over an ugly reality, as the sentimentalists of the Nineteenth Century had created a myth—critics were better able to understand the purpose of other, more ancient myths that southern writers were using to enrich their fables.

Louis D. Rubin, Jr., has provided the leanest summary of the first generation of twentieth-century southern fiction: "the period between 1925 and 1950 is most importantly William Faulkner's South." So large is the shadow that he cast, that any descendant writer has had a struggle "getting out from under William Faulkner," in Rubin's well-known phrase. But "another generation cometh," in the words of the Preacher: there have been about five hundred new southern novelists since 1940 (see appendix). And, by twisting the Preacher's sense, a reason for the need of another generation can be offered: "the earth abideth for ever." Such a vast claim will not be made for the South's future, which is bound to be short. But the South did last beyond Faulkner—or, to put it another way, even Faulkner was not able to use it all up. For the South was changing, far more and far faster than it ever had during his generation.

The most noticeable modulation is the loosening grip of history. Certainly historical novels based upon the myth continue to be written; a trip to the drug store suggests that any plantation gothic (especially if it puffs *Wind* in the title) is a sure-fire seller (especially if the house on the cover is framed by War-apocalyptic flames). But this genre proffers to modern tastes:

love (always genital, between races and sexes) in the ruins (of all conventions). There is far less of the intrustion of the past into the present in recent genuine southern novels; the frequency of images picturing the stable, traditional, religious life, in other words, steadily decreases. More and more the southerner seems to see himself as a product of present social complexities, not of past philosophic simplicities. And as he loses his preoccupation with himself as a victim of history, he seems to be turning his eyes outward to see for the first time the man with whom he has always shared the South—the black. And he is seeing him with greater clarity. The black is no longer the happy darky that he was in the sentimental novel; nor is he the tragic spectre, darkly suggestive of ancient guilt, that he was in many earlier novels of the renascence. Rather he is now viewed as a man—different from the white man, but man nevertheless. Or woman—for much of the best southern fiction in the past forty years has been written by women, black and white, about women, black and white.

The black, and the white southerner's response to him, has thus become one of the most important topics in recent southern fiction. This relationship was brilliantly depicted early, in Carson McCullers' *The Heart is a Lonely Hunter* (1940), in which a black shares the common lot; his heart is locked by pride, and he suffers the loneliness that must necessarily result. By the time of Shirley Ann Grau's *Keepers of the House* (1964) even the most taboo subject is open: in that novel the relationship between a white man and a black woman emphasizes their need for each other, not their affront to white society.

Such an emphasis identifies the pressing new concern in southern fiction—loneliness. As Louis D. Rubin, Jr., and Robert Jacobs long ago pointed out, the disintegration of society is no longer considered noteworthy by southern novelists. Now the concern is with the disintegration of the self. The southerner's life was once vitalized by his participation in the group, even though it meant sharing the collective guilt of the group. Now, however, the southerner must go it alone, and many of the best recent novels detail the failure of personality that occurs when one must go it alone. Again Carson McCullers's *The Heart is a Lonely Hunter* is an excellent example, with a title that anticipates a generation's quest. Other representatives are Truman Capote's *Other Voices, Other Rooms* (1948), William Styron's *Lie Down in Darkness* (1951), and Joan Williams's *The Morning and the Evening* (1961).

These new novels rely upon a radically different cluster of images. The recurrent actions of these works include murders, suicides, rapes, castrations, and self-mutilations. The recurrent characters include the insane, the idiotic, the obsessed, the freakish, and the perverted. Because of these elements, recent southern fiction has too often been dismissed as exercises in the gothic. But Tennessee Williams has accurately pointed out that these elements are the "externals" of fiction; they are only the images through which the "Sense of the Awful" can be communicated.

The celebration of the "Sense of the Awful" is not, though, an end in itself. On the contrary, the depiction of such actions and characters suggests a sense of optimism about the South. For, once these writers have made their point that life without some transcendent controlling principle is a shambles, they can begin to suggest, however tentatively, alternatives to such a life. All of them recognize that the southerner is now almost completely deprived of the help of tradition, custom, or community. It is the mode of survival that varies.

In the essays that follow, I trace some of the alternatives to despair offered by southern writers of "another generation." With twenty years of good scholarship in Flannery O'Connor now, my early (1965) essay about her use of the grotesque to express her Catholic vision seems to have weathered well. I suspect, though, that my contention that Richard Wright uses a Kierkegaardian pattern to detail his protagonist's quest for a traditional Christian belief is still controversial. With Harriette Arnow, I am happy to offer my reading that *The Dollmaker* describes a woman who, like Christ, accepts sacrifice as her life, to oppose those who see the story as a study in naturalism. William Styron's later novels do not reveal that he has advanced much beyond the belief that I trace in *Set This House on Fire*, that only faith can defeat despair; what he has not found is a ground for that faith. I am also happy to include a reading of Mitchell Jayne's novel, not merely to expand the geographical and racial range of my study, but to offer an appreciation of his theme: certainly an uncritical acceptance of the past (or what is accepted as the past) alienates a person, yet a discovery of the truth of the past strengthens that person to do what has to be done. It is fitting that the last essay deals with William Alexander Percy and Walker Percy—for William Alexander Percy, however much he may differ from Faulkner, is yet of the same generation, and Walker Percy, however much he may be a southern novelist, is nothing like Faulkner. Walker Percy's independence was not won without an enormous struggle—but this is not to say that he was ever tempted to treat Faulkner's South or to employ Faulkner's style. There was, though, that generation's vision: of man as the ultimate value and thus as an utter futility. With such a vision, inevitable defeat inhabits every victory, like a worm, and only the apocalypse can interrupt the decline. With a full appreciation for that generation's achievements, Walker Percy has firmly rejected its vision, to create another South, just as vital as Faulkner's, but thick with occasions of grace. Walker Percy thus offers the challenge to "another generation": if it is to get "out from under William Faulkner," it will have to see more in the South than he did. That more, to spell it out, must be the will, blessed by grace, which clears the ground for being, at the conclusion of Walker Percy's *The Second Coming*.[10]

[1] Southern writers accounted for twenty-eight best sellers before 1917, including three novels—*The Little Shepherd of Kingdom Come* and *The Trail of the Lonesome Pine*, by John Fox, Jr., and *The Crisis*, by Winston Churchill—that eventually sold more than a million copies apiece. Other very popular novels were Winston Churchill's *Richard Carvel* (750,000) and *Inside the Cup* (500,000)and Mary Johnston's *To Have and to Hold* (500,000). On the strength of Miss Johnston's popularity after *To Have and to Hold* (1900), advance orders for *Audrey* (1902) exceeded 100,000.

[2] Southern novelists of the twenties include: E. C. L. Adams, Carmen Barnes, Hamilton Basso, Jack Bethea, James Boyd, James Branch Cabell, Erskine Caldwell, Bowyer Campbell, Carl Carmer, Maristan Chapman, Eleanor Chilton, Irvin S. Cobb, Ruth Cross, Harris Dickson, Murrell Edmunds, Frank Elser, William Faulkner, Barry Fleming, John Fort, Lucy Furman, Ellen Glasgow, Isa Glenn, Edwin Granberry, Ward Greene, Corra Harris, Harris Hervey, DuBose Heyward, Donald Joseph, Edith Summers Kelley, Robert Emmet Kennedy, Harry Kroll, Morris Markey, George Madden Martin, James Stuart Montgomery, Frances Newman, Howard W. Odum, Stanley Olmstead, Fulton Ousler, Jennings Perry, Julia Peterkin, Edith Taylor Pope, Elizabeth Madox Roberts, Emanie Sachs, Dorothy Scarborough, Evelyn Scott, Hubert Shands, E. E. Sparling, Laurence Stallings, Wilbur Daniel Steele, T. S. Stribling, Fiswoode Tarleton, Jean Toomer, Lulu Vollmer, Lella Warren, Walter White, Ridley Wills, Thomas Wolfe, Clement Wood, and Stark Young.

[3] I wish to acknowledge John M. Bradbury's *Renaissance in the South* (Chapel Hill: University of North Carolina Press, 1963), which suggested many of the authors treated in this paper.

[4] Such works as James Stuart Montgomery's *Tall Men*, Morris Markey's *The Band Plays Dixie*, and James Boyd's *Marching On*, all published in 1927, reveal a notion of the complexity of history far beyond their predecessors.

[5] There is little of the local-color sentimentality of John Fox, Jr., or Mary Noailles Murfree in such works as Elizabeth Madox Roberts' stories of Kentucky, Stanley Olmstead's *At Top of Tobin* (1926) and DuBose Heyward's *Angel* (1926), both dealing with North Carolina, or the Tennessee fiction of Harry Kroll and Maristan Chapman.

[6] The institution of tenant farming and sharecropping is attacked in such novels as Hubert Shand's *White and Black* (1922), Edith Summers Kelley's *Weeds* (1922), Dorothy Scarborough's *In the Land of Cotton* (1923), and Jack Bethea's *Cotton* (1928). A sympathetic view of the strivings of lower class whites develops with such novels as Clement Wood's *Mountain* (1920), Ellen Glasgow's *One Man in His Time* (1922), Ruth Cross's *The Golden Cocoon* (1924), Elizabeth Madox Roberts' *The Time of Man* (1926), and Edwin Granberry's *Strangers and Lovers* (1928), The harshness with which the Southern community can deal with nonconformity is portrayed in Emanie Sach's *Talk* (1924) and T. S. Stribling's *Teeftallow* (1926) and *Bright Metal* (1928). Rather telling disapproval of Southern charm and gentility gone to seed is expressed in such novels as Ellen Glasgow's *The Romantic Comedians* (1926), Evelyn Scott's *Migrations* (1927), and Isa Glenn's *Southern Charm* (1928). Perhaps the most shocking novels to Southern sensibilities were those dealing with the myth of the Southern virgin; Frances Newman's *The Hard-Boiled Virgin* (1926), Ruth Cross's *The Unknown Goddess* (1926), and Edith Everett Taylor Pope's *Not Magnolia* (1928) suggest that Temple Drake's sisters shared her weaknesses and predilections.

[7] This intention to look realistically manifests itself in several ways. There is, for one thing, the Negro voicing his own individuality, as in Jean Toomer's *Cane* (1923) and Walter White's *Fire and the Flint* (1924) and *Flight* (1926). Then there is an interest in the folklore and legends of various groups of Negroes; Ambrose Gonzales' treatment of the Gullah dialect Negroes in *Black Border* (1922) and other collections of stories about the South Carolina coast is representative of this interest. Others are Robert Emmet Kennedy's *Black Cameo* (1924) and *Gritney People* (1927), which deal with the Louisiana Negro, and E. C. L. Adams' *Congaree Sketches* (1927) and *Nigger to Nigger* (1928), with a South Carolina setting. Howard W. Odum's *Rainbow Round My Shoulder* (1928) suggests a mythic prototype for the whole race. Still others treat the Negro as an individual, as in Mrs. George Madden Martin's *Children of the Mist* (1920), Clement Wood's *Nigger* (1922), T. S. Stribling's *Birthright* (1922), and DuBose Heyward's *Porgy*

(1925), which everyone remembers because of its stage production. Probably most memorable of all the treatments of the Negro in this period is the fiction of Mrs. Julia Peterkin—*Green Thursday* (1924), *Black April* (1927), and *Scarlet Sister Mary* (1928), the latter a best seller which received the Pulitzer Prize.

[8] This essay contained the seeds of Cash's well-known *The Mind of the South*.

[9] Southerners who published first novels during the thirties include: Lily Alexander, Eugene Armfield, Anne Armstrong, Harriette Arnow, William Attaway, John Peale Bishop, Arna Bontemps, Jack Boone, Gwen Bristow, Harriet Castlin, Brainard Cheney, Richard Coleman, Foxhall Daingerfield, Clifford Dowdey, H. J. Eckenrode, Willie Snow Ethridge, Roy Flannagan, Frances Fox, Charles Givens, Emily Godchaux, Caroline Gordon, Emmet Gowan, Paul Green, Bernice K. Harris, Harriett Hassell, Harlan Hatcher, Annette Heard, George Henderson, Pendleton Hogan, Stanley Hopkins, Zora Neale Hurston, Gerald W. Johnson, Wilbourne Kelley, George W. Lee, Harry Lee, Mary Linfield, Grace Lumpkin, Andrew Lytle, Horace McCoy, William March, Charles Martin, Julian Meade, E. K. Means, Gilmore Millen, Caroline Miller, Margaret Mitchell, Charles C. Munz, Blair Niles, E. P. O'Donnell, Myra Page, James Peery, George Sessions Perry, Green Peyton, Katherine Anne Porter, Marjorie Kinnan Rawlings, Robert Rylee, Thad St. Martin, Lyle Saxon, Charlie May Simon, Marie Stanley, Nan Bagby Stephens, Jesse Stuart, Waters Turpin, Howell Vines, Robert Penn Warren, Richard Wright, and Leane Zugsmith.

[10] Much of the original assertion of this essay (1967) has been superseded by the work of three masters of the field, C. Hugh Holman, Louis D. Rubin, Jr., and Lewis P. Simpson, and by several younger scholars, Richard Gray, *The Literature of Memory* (1977), Michael O'Brien, *The Idea of the American South* (1979), Richard H. King, *A Southern Renaissance* (1980), and Daniel J. Singal, *The War Within* (1983). But my newly appended conclusion—that Southern fiction must continue to fight its way toward a vision of life made vital by Christianity or die—has not received wide consideration. Marion Montgomery's brilliant trilogy will, I am confident, make an eloquent statement of the argument.

Wise Blood
and the Grotesque

*O*ffering itself as the most grotesque work in all of southern fiction, Flannery O'Connor's *Wise Blood* is a novel only in the widest possible sense of the word. It is a prose fiction of considerable length, but beyond that requirement none of the standard elements of the novel is to be found. The development of character, the exploration of character interaction, and the development of plot are unimportant. Such action as occurs is often without motivation, leads nowhere, and is almost always absurd. Any resemblance to the world of objective reality is certainly incidental. Yet, when these things are said, the book still remains one of the most impressive creations of the School of the Grotesque, or School of Southern Gothic. That the book is rewarding despite its unconventionality can be attributed to the author's singular vision and style. Miss O'Connor several times commented upon her vocation: her mission, as she saw it, was to depict the reality of Christianity to an audience for whom nothing transempircal is real. She wrote, "I don't think you should write something as long as a novel around anything that is not of the gravest concern to you and everybody else and for me this is always the conflict between an attraction for the Holy and the disbelief in it that we breathe in with the air of the times." Her style, it follows, is effective only if it serves her intention. She was uninterested in the felicities of the art of conventional fiction, and felt completely free to use absurdity, paradox, and illogicality, if those were the only media which would carry her vision.

The main character of *Wise Blood,* the Tennessean Haze Motes, is an example of the complete artistic freedom which Miss O'Connor allowed herself. Uninterested in creating a rounded character, she concentrated instead upon constructing a caricature whose flatness continually reminds us that he is unreal. To the charge that such a technique weakened her fiction, Miss O'Connor would have replied that any other technique would weaken her vision. She had no interest in Haze Motes as a human being; he was conceived, and his creator would have insisted that he remain, as an exemplum, as a vehicle whose attitudes and actions would personify a spiritual view which she wished to reveal. To make sure that we view Haze properly, she twice describes him as a puppet: "He looked as if he were held by a rope caught in the middle of his back and attached to the train ceiling." "He had the look of being held there, as if by an invisible hand, as if, if the hand lifted up, the figure would spring across the pool in one leap without the expression on his face changing once."

There are suggestions at times that the structure of the gospels is consciously being used: an abstract idea will first be introduced and then made concrete, as in the parables of Christ. Haze Motes was, in his creator's eyes, an exemplification of the deadly effect that southern fundamentalism could have on the soul, warping and terrorizing it so completely with its perversion of Christian doctrine that the soul in rebellion rejects entirely the idea of orthodox Christianity. Since the creation of a character whose premise lay in normality and logicality would encourage us to identify with him and thus blunt the effectiveness of her attack, Miss O'Connor wisely felt free to make her foil as bizarre, as distasteful, as ridiculous, as she thought necessary. In a day when she saw such actions and attitudes as Haze Motes represents taken for normal behavior, she felt that only by extreme departure from what is expected in both content and style could her characterization achieve its goal. As she said, "The novelist with Christian concerns will find in modern life distortions which are repugnant to him, and his problem will be to make these appear as distortions to an audience which is used to seeing them as natural; and he may well be forced to take ever more violent means to get his vision across to this hostile audience."

Miss O'Connor takes very little time sketching the background of Haze Motes. His mother is described: "She wore black all the time and her dresses were longer than other women's . . . She had a cross-shaped face and hair pulled close to her head." His grandfather is mentioned: ". . . a circuit preacher, who had ridden over three counties with Jesus hidden in his head like a stinger." These two people are representatives of the guilt-obsessed culture which terrified Haze so completely as a child that he had walked in shoes filled with stones. One of his first utterances in the novel, offered casually to a woman on a train, reveals that he is its true heir: "I reckon you think you been redeemed."

In such a culture, where Calvin, though probably unknown to most of its members, is more influential than Christ, guilt overshadows love as the quintessential aspect of Christianity, and Christianity has more an Old Testament flavor than a New. The preacher then assumes a somewhat Mosaic role of wrathful pursuer, hunting man down to confront him with the absolute sinfulness of his condition. And, emphasizing guilt, the fundamentalist preacher seems to find his motive force more often in hatred and vindictiveness than in love and charity. Whatever the source of his power, he is a man much admired, for he has power and prestige, and much feared, for he is a constant reminder that a day of reckoning will come. As Haze's grandfather shouted to man, "Jesus would have him in the end!"

With such familial and cultural influences, Haze early decides upon two courses of action: he will be a preacher, but he will avoid Jesus Christ, in his mind "a wild ragged figure motioning him to turn around and come off into the dark where he was not sure of his footing, where he might be walking on the water and not know it and then suddenly know it and drown." In his reasoning, if he can successfully deny Christ, then he can also deny man's original sin: "There was no Fall because there was nothing to fall from and no Redemption because there was no Fall and no Judgment because there wasn't the first two." To Miss O'Connor the reality of Christ was the idea underlying all preaching; the idea of what is to be preached is implicit in the idea of preaching. As a friend of Miss O'Connor, Sister Bernetta, has put it, ". . . most crucial of all (the adjective is a pertinent one) in understanding what constitutes a Catholic writer is the realization that for such a person history leads up to and away from what happened on Calvary the first Good Friday. The center of all Catholic fiction is the Redemption."

In Haze Motes, then, Miss O'Connor deliberately constructed an oxymoron as character. In this manner she escaped the danger inherent in using a caricature: that it will become predictable once its mannerisms are known. Since by nature there is an unavoidable tension between the mutually contradictory elements of an oxymoron, Haze Motes has a vitality that will last either until one element overcomes the other or until the tension destroys him.

The paradox at the center of her character's nature is further suggested by his name. Originally, when an early draft of part of the novel was published, Haze's surname was "Weaver." But "Motes" suggests Christ's injunction, in the King James Version of the Sermon on the Mount (Matthew vii, 3–5), against officious intrusion:

> And why beholdest thou the mote that is in thy brother's eye, but considerest not the beam that is in thine own eye?
> Or how wilt thou say to thy brother, Let me pull out the mote out of thine eye; and, behold, a beam *is* in thine own eye?
> Thou hypocrite, first cast out the beam out of thine own eye; and then shalt thou see clearly to cast out the mote out of thy brother's eye.

The name "Haze" also suggests that Miss O'Connor wished her character to be conceived as one of cloudy vision who nevertheless insolently attempts to guide others.

Nor was Miss O'Connor content in making Haze's name a reproach against his belief. At another point she undercuts him with irony when he pleads for his belief: "'Look at me!' Haze Motes cried, with a tare in his throat, 'and you look at a peaceful man! Peaceful because my blood has set me free. Take counsel from your blood and come into the Church Without Christ and maybe somebody will bring us a new jesus and we'll all be saved by the sight of him!'" As Miss O'Connor well knew, in the parable of the tares (Matthew xiii), Christ defines the tares as the "children of the wicked one." In fact, the enemy that sowed the tares is said to be the devil (Matthew, xiii, 39).

Since Miss O'Connor's main purpose in *Wise Blood* was to warn against defective spiritual vision, it seems almost inescapable that one of the most effective themes of the book is that of sight versus blindness. Its first sentence describes the demobilized Haze, on his way to Taulkinham, sitting at a forward angle on the green plush train seat, suggesting at once his intensity and the possibility that his sight may be impaired. Physical sight becomes associated with spiritual vision soon afterward, when we are told that Haze had used his mother's glasses to read the Bible. He had taken the glasses with him when he was drafted, and he had put them on the first time that he had felt he was being led into temptation, to preach to his tempters. Before he was discharged, "he had all the time he could want to study his soul in and assure himself that it was not there." Thereafter, he puts aside the glasses.

On his second night in Taulkinham, Haze meets a "blind" street preacher, an incident that allowed Miss O'Connor to establish a thematic paradox that continues throughout the novel: those without sight can see and those with sight cannot see, an echo of Christ's words (John ix, 39): ". . . I am come into the world, that they which see not might see; and that they which see might be made blind." The "blind" preacher, Asa Hawks, and his daughter move off down the street, and Haze, in his obsession to taunt the preacher about his beliefs, walks across the street against the light, endangering his life and angering the policeman there. When the policeman sarcastically inquires if Haze knows the purpose of the signal light, Haze replies, "I didn't see it." Here again Haze's obsession with religious delusion, to the exclusion of everything else in the world around him, is suggested by his defective and inattentive sight.

When Haze catches up with the pair, he is told to pass out fundamentalist pamphlets for them, as a crowd pours out of an auditorium. But that command is abhorrent: "I'll take them up there and throw them over into the bushes! . . . You be watching and see can you see." The "blind" man replies, "I can see more than you . . . You got eyes and see not, ears and hear not, but you'll have to see some time," echoing Christ's words (Mark viii, 18): "Having eyes, see ye not? and having ears, hear ye not? . . ." The irony of the "blind" preacher's words operates on both a superficial and a profound level; physically he can in fact see, and spiritually Haze will not see until he has blinded himself. Raging because of the preacher's words, Haze begins himself to preach to the emerging crowd: "Listen here, I'm a preacher myself and I preach the truth . . . Don't I have eyes in my head? Am I a blind man?" Again as Miss O'Connor well knew, in terms of Christ's words to the Pharisees (John ix, 41), who were also denying His reality, Haze is not blind: "If ye were blind ye should have no sin: but now ye say, We see; therefore your sin remaineth."

The ancient forty-dollar rat-colored Essex that Haze buys also contributes to the theme of blindness versus sight. The car comes to represent Haze's attitude of deliberately wishing not to accept the reality of Christ. As he tells Sabbath Lily Hawks, the "blind" preacher's ugly daughter, "Nobody with a good car needs to be justified." Then he voices his need for the car: "I knew when I first saw it that it was the car for me, and since I've had it, I've had a place to be that I can always get away in." And from its hood Haze preaches his perverted vision.

His reliance upon the car for escape is especially clear in a scene after Sabbath seduces him. Always before, Haze had considered himself guiltless of sin, for how could one be sinful if one did not believe in redemption? But Sabbath teaches him how to be sinful: "Yes sir! . . . I like being that way, and I can teach you how to like it." Haze does. The next morning he is described "lying on his cot," however, "with a washrag over his eyes; the exposed part of his face . . . ashen and set in a grimace, as if he were in some permanent pain." The washrag foreshadows his blinding of himself, when he has come to see. The triumphant Sabbath then enters to show Haze the dried, shrunken corpse, which Enoch Emery had stolen from the museum, in answer to Haze's pleas for someone to give him a new jesus. Just as Sabbath enters, Haze has decided to leave; he begins to pack his duffel bag, accidentally touching the case with his mother's glasses in it, and he stops for a moment to put them on. When Haze sees the mummy through his mother's glasses, his response is so violent and apparently absurd that it can only have symbolic meaning. To see any jesus through his mother's glasses would be to accept the guilt that her religion emphasized and that he had rejected. He flings the new jesus out of doors and the glasses right behind it, refusing to look, for, as he chokes out, "I don't want nothing but the truth! . . . and what you see is the truth and I've seen it! . . . I've seen the only truth there is!" And when Sabbath asks his destination, he shouts, "To some other city, . . . to preach the truth. The Church Without Christ! And I got a car to get there in, . . ."

Before Haze attempts to flee the city, he murders Solace Layfield, whose Puritan name suggests what he represents. One night on the street Haze had preached, "Your conscience is a trick . . . it don't exist though you may think it does, and if you think it does, you had best get it out in the open and hunt it down and kill it, because it's no more than your face in the mirror is or your shadow behind you." At that moment a double-figure, the True Prophet, Solace Layfield, who works for the confidence man Hoover Shoats, is introduced. The resemblance between the two is so striking that a woman asks Haze, "Him and you twins?" And Haze, watching Solace, in *his* glare-blue suit preaching from the hood of *his* rat-colored car, furiously replies: "If you don't hunt it down and kill it, it'll hunt you down and kill you." The night after his seduction, Haze follows Solace home. When the two cars reach the countryside, Haze demolishes the car by forcing it off the road, and Solace, uninjured, comes back to the window of the Essex to ask, "It ain't nothing wrong with that car . . . Howcome you knockt it in the tich?" Haze replies, "You ain't true, . . . What do you get up on top of that car and say you don't believe in what you believe in for? . . . You ain't true, . . . You believe in Jesus." Haze then runs Solace down with his car to kill him. Again apparently meaningless violence has symbolic meaning. Both the True Prophet and the Essex are objectified mental attitudes: Haze's deliberate attempt not to see the truth (the Essex) is still able to overcome his conscience (the double, Solace Layfield), in which remain his childhood guilt and belief in the reality of Christ.

The next morning, beginning his trip to the new city, Haze stops at a filling station, where he tells an attendant who questions the condition of his car that "nobody with a good car needed to worry about anything." His words quickly prove to be untrue, for he runs afoul of the law for the second time; as soon as he reaches the highway, a patrolman, with an apparently meaningless act, orders Haze out of his car, which is then pushed over a cliff. "Was you going anywheres?" he asks Haze, and when Haze answers, "No," the patrolman even repeats the question: "'You hadn't planned to go anywheres?' Haze shook his head. His face didn't change and he didn't turn it toward the patrolman. It seemed to be concentrated on space." This Saul does not become a Paul; with his hope of denying Christ gone, Haze returns to the city, there to blind himself, as a sign that he can now see his guilt.

With the theme of deliberate self-delusion concluded, the theme of blindness versus vision continues, to end, as it had begun, the novel. People other than Sabbath Lily had noticed Haze's eyes. The woman on the train, Mrs. Wally Bee Hitchcock, had also scrutinized them: "Their settings were so deep that they seemed, to her, almost like passages leading somewhere and she leaned across the space that separated the two seats, trying to see into them." Trying to see into Haze's eyes is repeated when Haze's landlady is fascinated by his self-inflicted blindness and his other punishments of the body. She asks why he walks with rocks in his shoes, and when he answers that he must pay, she persists, "But what have you got to show that you're paying for?" Fully conscious now of the paradoxical truth of Christ's words, ". . . I am come into the world, that they which see not might see; and that they which see might be made blind," Haze answers, "Mind your business, . . . You can't see." From then on, the landlady is obsessed with his scarred eye sockets, and after his murder by the two policemen the novel ends with a description of her final attempt to fathom them: "She sat staring with her eyes shut, into his eyes, and felt as if she had finally got to the beginning of something she couldn't begin, and she saw him moving farther and farther away, farther and farther into the darkness until he was the pin point of light."

As I have indicated, much of the action of the novel is at first apparently extraneous, excessively violent, and meaningless. The plot, such as it is, relates the story of Haze Motes' unsuccessful attempt to fight off a belief in Christ; it is buried, however, in a welter of extraneous action that almost always has an unexpected outcome, sometimes quite hilarious and often gruesome. The novel immediately suggests the quest notif, but when Haze returns home after demobilization, the only thing which happens to him is that a board falls on him during the night. Haze's quest is further mocked, when he steps out on the platform at one stop and misses the train. Finally, the ridiculousness of the quest is confirmed, when Haze, arriving at Taulkinham, has no place to go, until he sees the name of Mrs. Leora Watts on a lavatory wall: "The friendliest bed in town! Brother." And so on, throughout the novel, one unexpectedness follows another: the blind see, the innocent are guilty, and the clean are unclean. When Haze first starts his car, it is naturally in reverse gear. When a "gorilla" is led out to meet people in front of a theatre, it refuses to perform until it is given a raincoat.

Character relationships are equally meaningless and abortive. Haze meets the "blind" preacher, and apparently the predominant conflict of the book is to be between these two, until the preacher leaves town to take a job on a banana boat. Enoch Emery appears in a fairly large portion of the novel, but he wanders off to steal a gorilla suit, in which he scares people rather than making friends as he had expected. Sabbath Lily Hawks is placed in a juvenile detention ward. Onnie Jay Holy, Haze's first disciple, becomes Hoover Shoats, the confidence man, and then he, too, disappears. Solace Layfield appears only long enough to be murdered.

There is, then, really only one character; the others are personifying figures, used as exempla and then dropped. And in Miss O'Connor's aesthetic, this method was the only one which would not weaken her vision. If any of these figures were rounded and involved in a meaningful conflict with Haze, the emphasis in the book would be upon man's relation to man, whereas in Miss O'Connor's view, the only reason for writing a novel is to explore man's dependence upon Christ.

If the content of *Wise Blood* seems bizarre and ludicrous, the rhetoric only reinforces that appearance. Extremely incongruous images, oxymorons, and synesthesia convince us that here indeed is a strange new world. Objects are like humans and animals, human beings are like animals and insects, and animals are like human beings. But the unconventional rhetoric is not an embellishment pasted upon a basically conventional view of the world. It is indeed a warped world, one which has been likened to a Chagall painting, and the comparison of the novel to the modern painting seems especially apt for Miss O'Connor often appears to share modern painting's preoccupations. Her world frequently is that of a dream (in keeping with her topsy-turvy aesthetic, dreams are perhaps the most lucid and conventional parts of the book), with characters who transpose themselves, with aimless action endlessly performed, with bizarre mixtures of the known and the unfamiliar. Surrealistically, soda fountain chairs are "brown toad stools," trees look "as if they had on ankle-socks," and a cloud has "curls and a beard" before it becomes a bird. The physical world partakes of the strangeness which colors character and action: the sky leaks and growls, the wind slashes around the house, "making a sound like sharp knives swirling in the air," and "the sky was like a piece of thin polished silver with a dark sour-looking sun in one corner of it."

Miss O'Connor believed that it was her Catholicism which prompted her to describe the world as a bizarre and sinister dream: "My own feeling is that writers who see by the light of their Christian faith will have, in these times, the sharpest eyes for the grotesque, for the perverse, and for the unacceptable." She further thought that such a specific vantage point suggested the themes with which she worked: "I will admit to certain preoccupations that I get, I suppose, because I'm a Catholic; preoccupations with belief and with death and grace and the devil." But while belief and grace offered spiritual incentive to her writing, death and the devil offered the human terrors which make fiction remarkable. "I'm a born Catholic," she said, "and death has always been a brother to my imagination. I can't imagine a story that doesn't properly end in it or in its foreshadowings." Her statement is borne out by the fact that *Wise Blood* begins and ends with a *memento mori:* "The outline of a skull under his skin was plain and insistent" and "The outline of a skull was plain under his skin and the deep burned eye sockets seem to lead into the dark tunnel where he had disappeared."

But, for all that has been said, there may linger a suspicion that content and form are not joined in *Wise Blood.* Nearly everyone who has commented on the novel has noticed the malformed characterizations, the complete absurdity of action and event, and other features which depart from convention. Is it not, then, a far-fetched story, which the author has attempted to dignify by grafting on a highly unconventional rhetoric? I think not. Given the author's many statements of her intentions, we must assume that she would have expected her work to be judged by its communicability, and would not have departed from the conventional structure and treatment of the novel, if she had thought innovations in style or absurdities in content would detract from her vision.

I have suggested elements of symbolism which seem to join content and form and which give qualities of coherency and unity to the work, but I believe that there is yet a motif to be traced which serves first as an ironic and then as a serious basis for the conception of Haze Motes, a motif which serves as a coagulant for the diverse aspects of the work. If one cannot create the perfect form perhaps the next best thing is to create the perfect deformity. Satirists have always chosen the latter course, and that seems to have been Miss O'Connor's choice. In her view, the only conflict that would sustain for her a work as long as a novel was that of belief versus disbelief. She could have, then, chosen to narrate the story of a modern saint. But such a story would have had the quality of sentimental and intrusive moralism, of preaching, about it which would have alienated the very audience which she wanted to reach. She could have, then, chosen to analyze the rather normal man's attempt to establish a meaningful spiritual relationship in a world where disbelief, especially in the guise of belief, is rampant. But the trouble with this approach would be that the character might be so like his audience that it would not have perceived his problem. That leaves, then, the opposite of the saint: the active disbeliever. Here a demonic figure could have been constructed, but a demonic figure would be without the desire to believe in the first place, and so there would have been no conflict. The ideal figure, it seems, would be a saint who disbelieved, that is, one who was actively searching for religious meaning (as opposed to the majority who passively accept the traditional view although they secretly regard it as nonsense) but who did not find it in the established beliefs.

What would be better, then, than to posit the form first and then let the character grow to fit it? In this manner the possibility of ironical treatment is available at first, when the character differs completely from the form, when he does the right thing for the wrong reason. Then, as the character is inevitably forced into the form, it receives straight-forward treatment; rather than work by opposites the author can then work by similarities, thus effecting the supreme irony: the only possibility of actively rejecting an idea to which the majority pays lip-service is through the same behavior as that of actively accepting the idea, that is, both disbeliever and believer are "outsiders," in that they seriously think about their spiritual life, whereas most people are so immersed in a materialistic life that they neither accept nor reject religion.

The legend of St. Anthony could be the form. An Egyptian monk of the third century who was evidently a visionary, Anthony gave up his worldly property to go into the desert to live as an ascetic. Here the Devil, often in the guise of animals, continually tempted him. The Temptation of St. Anthony early became an attractive subject for painters who wished to depict man in conflict with the demonic; painters from Martin Schoengauer to Salvadore Dali have utilized the legend. Nor have painters alone been fascinated by the possibilities of the legend; both Flaubert and Faulkner found it compelling.

Haze Motes at first seems an unlikely St. Anthony figure. But the wide differences in time and place become unimportant when the essentially similar natures of the two men are seen. Both are possessed with an overpowering sense of the importance of religious belief as the only force which can give order and meaning to their lives. And both use self-abasement to express their relization of the gulf which separates the human from the spiritual. One accepts a saint as a flagellant, but one is at first surprised that Haze Motes, the illiterate Tennesseean, unconsciously knows of the centuries-old method of chastising the flesh to purify the soul.

Once the suggestion is implanted that Haze is to be regarded seriously as a seeker after divine truth, rather than as just another Bible-beating southerner, the departure from the form is begun. Whereas Anthony had renounced civilization to find God in the desert, it is in the desert that Haze finds his substitute for God; the army "sent him to another desert and forgot him again. He had all the time he could want to study his soul in and assure himself that it was not there." And where Anthony's confrontation with God had left him humble, Haze's false truth goads him into pride; his actions at first betray his contemptuousness of other people, who may believe in the fiction that he has discarded, but soon his words reveal the prideful unbeliever: "'I'm going to do some things I never have done before,' he said and gave her a sidelong glance and curled his mouth slightly."'

Haze also departs from the form when he seeks the city; "God made the country but man made the town" is at least as old as St. Augustine, but for Miss O'Connor, who always conceives of the city as Sodom, such a moral geography is still valid. When Haze reaches the city, his life once again parallels St. Anthony's; according to the legend, St. Anthony was subjected to harassment by all sorts of demons, and the invention of all kinds of demonic forms became the distinguishing characteristic of paintings which used the Temptation as a subject. Haze, too, is bordered on all sides by monsters. With figure of speech, with description, and even with suggestive names—Hawks, Shoats—the author emphasizes that Haze has plunged himself into a chaos filled with every kind of monstrous apparition.

All of the characters have some animalistic aspect to their natures, and all represent some type of worldly threat to Haze's unworldly quest. Hawks is the fake preacher, unable at the moment of truth to act in the name of that which he had preached. Sabbath Lily Hawks is the complete sensualist, who recognizes that Haze is obsessed: "I knew when I first seen you you were mean and evil, . . . I seen you wouldn't let nobody have nothing. I seen you were mean enough to slam a baby against the wall. I seen you wouldn't never have no fun or let anybody else because you didn't want nothing but Jesus." And Hoover Shoats, who had posed as Onnie Jay Holy, is Haze's special tempter; like the pig which is generally shown in depictions of St. Anthony as a figure symbolic of sensuality and gluttony, the worst threats to his attempts to lead the religious life, Shoats is the particularly twentieth-cenury, bourgeois threat to Haze's religious vision; he sees the commercial possibilities of

Haze's belief and he wants to make a confidence game it: "'Now I just want to give you folks a few reasons why you can trust this church—'"

Once the tension between the form, St. Anthony, and the departure from it, Haze Motes, has been established, there is little need for its constant emphasis. Rather, the novel is a series of events, or panels of a painting as it were, showing Haze being tormented by the symbolically-different weird beasts. The motif is not reintroduced until near the end of the novel, when Haze has been forced to see that there is no escape from Christ. Structurally, of course, it is at this point when the departure from the form becomes the form. For the description of Haze's final, saint-like actions, the point of view is shifted to the eyes of Haze's horsy, love-sick landlady. After the destruction of his car, of his delusion, Haze returns to blind himself. Thereafter his landlady, mainly because of his large disability check (which is one hundred per cent and suggests that Haze was a mentally exhausted victim of the war), takes great interest in Haze and observes him closely: "He could have been dead and get all he got out of life but the exercise. He might as well be one of them monks, she thought, he might as well be in a monkery." When she learns that Haze walks in shoes filled with rocks and broken glass and wears strands of barbed wire wrapped around his chest, she is convinced of his insanity: "'Well, it's not normal. It's like one of them gory stories, it's something that people have quit doing—like boiling in oil or being a saint or walling up cats, . . .'"

Miss O'Connor was fully conscious that her work lay within a "school of the grotesque." She made several remarks about the presence of the grotesque in her art. Though she felt that modern life has made grotesques of us all, still, she thought that too often her work was termed "grostesque" when she had no intention of achieving that response. She justified her use of it as the only mode of illusion through which she could reach her audience. I doubt that she would have attempted a rigid definition for "grotesque"; she had used the term in too many contexts. I do believe, however, that her purpose in using it can be safely stated: the grotesque for her was a form of religious hyperbole. There is always the danger that an audience not attuned to the form will misunderstand such hyperbole. That is the chance that Miss O'Connor must have felt she had to take. Certainly she was deadly serious when she used the grotesque, and its use was not merely gratuitous. Just as certainly she was not merely celebrating southern degeneracy.

Flannery O'Connor was, on the contrary, perhaps the writer of the modern southern school most conscious of the chaotic world caused by the declining belief in older religious institutions. Thus her satire was the most desperate, for to her it was most obvious that the old order was crumbling. But she saw that the old order in religion remained a husk; therefore she had to attack those people who play out their lives within the old form without giving allegiance to it and those people who have gone over more obviously to some other allegiance. There was no place in her world for any norms; from her vantage point the entire world did look grotesque, since her audience did not recognize the normative value of faith.

Cross Damon:
Kierkegaardian Man of Dread

*A*lthough most critics argue that Richard Wright derives much of the conceptual material for his fable in *The Outsider* (1953) from Camus and Sartre, Kingsley Widmer notes that he also employs the "organizing concept of Kierkegaardian "dread'."[1] But while Widmer mentions the influence of Kierkegaard in the novel, he apparently does not regard it as a significant factor, for he mentions it only in passing. If anything, Widmer feels that a rigid adherence to ideas from Kierkegaard damages the structure of the novel. A close analysis of Wright's use of Kierkegaard's work, especially *The Concept of Dread,* is helpful, however, in demonstrating that Wright is offering essentially a Christian, rather than an atheistic existential view.

Entitled "Dread," the first section of the novel contains the motto: "Dread is an alien power which lays hold of an individual, and yet one cannot tear oneself away, nor has a will to do so; for one fears what one desires."[2] This quotation is cited in the "Introduction by the Translator" of the American edition of *The Concept of Dread,*[3] and very probably Wright found it there. The same idea in slightly different form appears in the body of that work, and the context surrounding it there helps the reader to understand the dialectical way in which Cross Damon must be viewed and prepares the reader for the final statement by that dying murderer: "in my heart . . . I'm . . I felt . . . I'm *innocent.* . . . That's what made the horror . . ." (440, *sic*). The immediate context of the quotation is: "The qualitative leap is outside of ambiguity, but he who through dread becomes guilty is innocent, for it was not he himself but dread, an alien power, which laid hold of him, a power he did not love but dreaded— and yet he is guilty, for he sank in the dread which he loved even while he feared it."[4]

However much he may wish to deny it, Cross was born with a Christian heritage. His mother, steeped in the traditional Christianity of the Mississippi Negro, moans in dismay at what her son has become: "To think I named you Cross after the Cross of Jesus" (23). He himself thinks that his mother's transmission to him really amounted to an unmerited sense of guilt: "His adolescent fantasies had symbolically telescoped this God into an awful face shaped in the form of a huge and crushing NO, a terrifying face which had, for a reason he could not learn, created him, had given him a part of Himself and yet had threateningly demanded that he vigilantly deny another part of himself which He too had paradoxically given him" (18).

As a child Cross had attempted to reject this burden of original sin that apparently so completely separated body from soul. Unable to find the grounds of his guilt, he attempted to free himself from his sense of guiltiness. If he could will himself to disbelieve the idea which he had inherited with his very life, if he could will himself to believe in his innocence, then he would be an Adam before the Fall. And there is that part of him which believes in his fundamental innocence even to the moment of his death. One part of the dialectic of his life is buried in his surname: in *Damon* is *Adam* the innocent.[5]

Innocence, according to Kierkegaard, is also dread, however: "This is the profound secret of innocence, that at the same time it is dread."[6] And Cross realizes that he can be both innocent and in dread: "He was aware, intimately and bitterly, that his dread had been his mother's first fateful gift to him. He had been born of her not only physically but emotionally too" (17). His childhood and adolescence had consequently been conditioned by a state of acute, but unlocalized dread: "Afraid of what? Nothing exactly, precisely . . . And this constituted his sense of dread" (18, *sic*).

In such a state of innocence/dread, Cross had imagined the Christian God as the wrathful and prohibitive dictator: "This God's NO-face had evoked in his pliable boy's body an aching sense of pleasure by admonishing him to shun pleasure as the tempting doorway opening blackly onto hell; had too early awakened in him a sharp sense of sex by thunderingly denouncing sex as the sin leading to eternal damnation; had posited in him an unbridled hunger for the sensual by branding all sensuality as the monstrous death from which there was no resurrection; had made him instinctively choose to love himself over and against all others because he felt himself menaced by a mysterious God Whose love seemed somehow like hate" (18).

Prohibition awakens the possibility of freedom; if this wrathful God orders him *not* to act, he will make every effort not to act—but then there lingers in his mind the subtle hint that if God has to *order* him not to act, then he *could* act, if he wished. Torn in this way, Cross becomes a young man both celibate, in adherence to the thunderings of that commandment, and yet lustful, in response to the desire that his sinfulness posits in him. At the same time he is drawn into the study of philosophy in college, hoping to find a system to replace the "NO-face" that induces such dreadful traps. He himself realizes that desire and philosophy as objects of his quest both have the same origin: "Ideas had been his only sustained passion, but he knew that his love of them had that same sensual basis that drew him achingly to the sight of a girl's body swinging in a tight skirt along a sunny street" (49).

When Cross marries Gladys, it would appear that his problems would be resolved. His sexual needs could now be safely met, in the Christian institution of marriage. His loneliness and self-doubt could be combatted by the companionship of his wife and any children they might produce. Ironically, however, the arrival of his first child marks the time when it becomes apparent that he will not be able to live by the conventions adopted by his society. While his wife is in the hospital he allows desire to overcome him, so that his wife arrives home to find him in bed with a prostitute whom he had picked up at some point during his drunken celebration of the birth of Cross, Jr.

The defects of his dread-dominated personality are strikingly evident here. He betrays his wife, just as he is, in one way or another, to betray every other woman whom he meets in the remainder of his life. But this is not to say that Cross is a monster at this time who suffers no remorse or who has no wish to live a different kind of life. On the contrary, his personality is engulfed with self-hatred (56). Thus his fractured personality wars within itself, as he fights both to observe and yet at the same time transgress the morality imposed upon him.

Through his initiative the marriage founders, and Cross becomes the irresponsible seducer, having forgotten now his plans for a college education, able only to maintain his job at the post office and to attempt burying his self-loathing in immediacy by bouts of drunkenness and sensuality. Though the attempt to find escape in sensuality always fails, he continues to seek absolute immediacy in the pursuit of "woman as body of woman . . ." (30), as Wright terms the object of Cross's sexual propensity, which in reality represents the possibility of freedom. At the same time Cross persists in a "habit of incessant reflection . . ." (17), a habit which mirrors, according to Kierkegaard, the dread existing in a personality.[7]

In time he comes across a new feminine body, Dot Powers, to be struck at once by a desire so urgent that "his head felt pleasantly giddy . . ." (30). Even as he first tentatively fondles her, he is reflective enough to observe the state which he induces in her: "He noticed that she was trembling slightly and he knew that she was being claimed by a state he knew well: dread . . ." (31). In his diagnosis of Dot's condition here Cross is relying upon the Kierkegaard that he has read. For in treating the capacity of women for dread Kierkegaard writes: "If I picture to myself a young and innocent girl and then let a man fasten upon her a look of desire, she experiences dread."[8] As an image of possibility, the youthful Dot is of great attractiveness to Cross, and he takes her as his mistress.

It is only a matter of months before she announces to Cross that she is pregnant, but even before her announcement Cross has admitted to himself that he is already tired of her (25). For he knows that in desiring her he had really only desired desire, had really only desired possibility. Now that she has in fact become the image of entrapment, ready to saddle him with the same responsibilities that he had so recently eluded, Dot is the last person in the world whom he wishes to acknowledge. Therefore, even though she threatens to leap to her death, he spurns her. Now he sees himself doubly trapped: even if he could get a divorce from Gladys, he would then be forced to marry Dot—or face the criminal suit that she, as a minor, could bring against him.

These are days of intense self-loathing. He is well-read enough to think of his fundamental problem as "one of the relationship of himself to himself . . ." (8), an analysis echoing the description of the disrelationship of despair offered by Kierkegaard in *The Sickness Unto Death:* "Despair is the disrelationship in a relation which relates itself to itself."[9] He will not admit, though, that this problem is ultimately of a religious dimension. In a simple but perceptive way, however, his friend Joe Thomas tells Cross as much: "It's between you and your Maker, your problem . . ." (8). Cross, though, can only envy Joe his ability to believe in what to Cross is a simplistic illusion. He can only despair over his self to the point of contemplating suicide, "of jumping through the jungle of problems that plagued him from within and from without" (13).

His entrapment seems complete. Caught in a life he cannot stand, but without the will to end it, fixed between two threatening figures of feminine possessiveness, he seems to be completely without resources. The subway wreck, however, sweeps away all previous considerations. By a fluke of luck, Cross has been offered the freedom that he has always sought: "All of his life he had been hankering after his personal freedom, and now freedom was knocking at his door, begging him to come in" (84). But if luck occasionally helps, it just as surely will hinder. When Cross finds a hotel where he can hide until it is safe to leave Chicago, he accidentally meets his old friend Joe Thomas in the hall. To Joe a miracle has occurred; he sees a man who has risen from the dead; thus a scene from the Scriptures is reenacted, with Joe as the Doubting Thomas and Cross as the risen Christ: "Speak, man! They say you're dead, but you ain't no ghost and I damm well know it! . . . I got to *touch* you to believe it!" (106). Joe is the very picture of the traditional Negro: jolly, optimistic, content in his belief in a personal Christian God. He cannot conceive that he is really looking at a new man, who must kill him in order to retain the freedom that he has chosen. Cross crushes Joe's skull, then topples him out the window. so that it will appear that Joe might have leaped to his death.

The act of murder could represent Cross's killing of his own past as a convention-abiding Negro postal worker in Chicago, since Joe was all of these. It could also symbolize Cross's rejection of the Christian belief held by Joe. But beyond these aspects it marks a further, fatal step in Cross's life history. For as Kierkgaard puts: "The history of the individual goes forward in a movement from state to state. Every state is posited by a leap. In this way sin comes into the world, and so does it continue to come, unless it is stopped. Yet every repetition of it is not a simple consequence but a new leap."[10] The first leap in the novel was only an imagined leap, a desire to jump "through the jungle of problems . . ." (13), a contemplation of self-destruction. The next leap in the novel, which was after all only a threatened leap by the betrayed Dot, turned out to have been of little consequence, even though it was a betrayal and hence a foreshadowing of Cross's future actions. Joe Thomas's "leap," though, turns the world against Cross and makes him a criminal in the eyes of society. The next leap, that by Eva, will turn Cross irrevocably against himself.

Even though he has killed Joe Thomas, Cross still views himself as an innocent victim. Near the moment of his own death he explains *his* version of Thomas' death: "I killed him . . . to keep him from . . . betraying me . . .' (438). To a subjectivity convinced of its own innocence and supremacy, such an interpretation of the act would be "realistic"; for as Kierkegaard puts it: "This is the profound secret of innocence, that at the same time it is dread. Dreamingly the spirit projects its own reality, but this reality is nothing, but this nothing constantly sees innocence outside of it."[11]

In the second section of the novel Cross becomes frantically aware that his spirit is tempting him to believe in the reality which it projects. Over and over on his train trip from Chicago to New York, Cross is conscious that his mind could easily trick him. As he sits waiting for his breakfast to be served, he senses his precarious mental state: "Out of a void, anxiety rose and captured his senses; he could feel the reality of the dining car falling away as his consciousness projected menacing meanings on the look of the world" (121–122). One part of him desperately wants to believe that the world is conspiring against him: "His sensibilities clamored to believe in this delusion; his emotions needed the certainty of this transparent fantasy; yet, in the end, his mind was tough enough to cling to its anchorage in the hard ambiguities of normal reality" (122).

At this time also, Cross begins to experience fully the nothingness that his act of murder had created: "Nothing made meaning; his life seemed to have turned into a static dream whose frozen images would remain unchanged throughout eternity" (102). It is thus quite fitting that this section is entitled "Dream."

Even with his occasional fits of awareness of the danger posed by his dread-filled spirit, it is still Cross's delusion that he can project a reality which will replace the reality accepted by other people: "What helped him most was that he possessed the lucky capacity of reducing and referring his memories to an intense and personal basis, and could, therefore, once he was emotionally free of the concrete context from which they had sprung, live with them without a too crushing sense of guilt" (118). He thinks that he can create for himself a new identity as easily as he assumes a new name. But each new assumed name seems exhausted by its use in a betrayal. Following the subway wreck he becomes "Charles Webb" when he registers at the hotel in Chicago, but after betraying Joe Thomas and the prostitute

Jenny he discards that name. The he becomes "Addison Jordan" on the train for New York, but his first act with the new name is yet another betrayal, this time of the dining car steward, Robert Hunter (131).

Wright indicates the lack of vitality of this name at the very moment of its birth by having "Addison Jordan" give as his address in New York what turns out to be the location of a funeral home. Since Hunter will not be able to find "Addison Jordan" to support his defense in the suit to be brought against him, he will lose his job. And Cross, realizing this, is deeply disturbed about his treachery: "His non-identity was making Hunter believe in the unreal. Cross sighed. He had to break out of this dream, or he would surely go mad. He had to be born again, come anew into the world. To live amidst others without an identity was intolerable" (132). When he arrives in New York, therefore, he is obsessed to create a new identity which will invest his personality once more with solidity and specification. The new personality will enable him to engage in relations with others, will, he hopes, thus authenticate him. For, as it is, he feels that his separation from the world has made problematic the reality of the world which he views: "It was this static dream world that had elicited those acts of compulsion, those futile attempts to coerce reality to his emotional demands" (143). He knows what will happen to him, if he cannot reestablish a connection with his environment: "Panic drapes the look of the world in strangeness, and the more one stares blankly at that world, the stranger it looks, the more hideously frightening it seems. There is then born in one a wild, hot wish to project out upon that alien world the world that one is seeking" (143–144).

Cross's elaborate attempt to create a new self is mocked with his very first effort; he goes to a cemetery ("*strictly* colored," 149) to find a new name, this one somehow sounding the phoniest yet: "Lionel Lane." One of his first acts with his new public person is to attempt to undo his treachery toward Bob Hunter, he visits Hunter, to discover that Hunter harbors no malice toward him because of the betrayal. Instead, Hunter is fired with zeal for his new job as an organizer for the Communist Party. At once he begins a campaign to interest Cross in his organization, and though the campaign is transparent, Cross agrees to meet Gil Blount, Bob's superior. When they meet, Cross is filled with bitter amusement at the first principle that Blount proclaims: "We Communists do not admit any subjectivity in human life, . . ." (174). But, although he is intensely aware of the falsity of that belief and thus of any philosophy or party depending upon it, Cross allows himself to be recruited. He feels that the demands placed upon his energies in defense of his individuality by such a grasping organization as the Party will cause him to regain his sense of vitality and relatedness. Book II concludes, then, with Cross's delusion that he has achieved the impossible: "The dream in which he had lived since he fled Chicago was leaving him. The reality about him was beginning to vibrate: he was slowly becoming himself again, but it was a different self" (186).

Book III has for a motto a quotation from St. Paul (Romans VII, 15): "For that which I do I allow not: for what I would, that I do not; but what I hate, that do I," This realization of human perversity accords closely with the statement by Kierkegaard that Wright chose as the motto for Book I. At this point Cross is precisely in this dialectical condition of being both innocent because dread impelled him to the act which resulted in his guilt and guilty because he passively sank deeper into dread. Even on the train Cross knows that he must gain self-control: "He had to master himself; he had to steer clear of being always drawn toward that which he dreaded" (136). Since the movement here is a drift into the depths of dread, Book III is called "Descent."

One of the conditions that Gil Blount imposes upon Cross's novitiate is that he reside in the Blount apartment. Thus he moves in, to become a pawn between Blount and his racist landlord, Herndon. His first encounter with Herndon reinforces his feeling that in crisis situations there is intensified reality: "The encounter with Herndon had given him a lift, had almost

made the last shred of dreaminess leave" (215). His second encounter with Herndon, when he murders both Herndon and
Blount just before one of them would have murdered the other,
completes his feeling of returning to a world of clear, precise
reality: "The universe seemed to be rushing at him with all its
totality. He was anchored once again in life, in the flow of things;
the world glowed with an intensity so sharp that it made his
body ache" (227).

After Cross fled Chicago, he lost that frantic desire for women
that was so much a part of his being. This loss of desire seems
symptomatic of his feeling of total loss of aliveness, which results
from his removal from his accustomed concrete placement and
from his reluctance to venture to hope, to possess ideals. Cross
knows that desire for desire is really desire for possibility, and
he never wants again to try to sublimate his desire through
eroticism: "—he wanted never again to seek fulfillment of desire
in that direction" (119). He seems determined to avoid the trap
offered by sexuality, for he quickly stifles his response to Mrs.
Turner, his first landlady in New York: "woman as body of
woman shot through his senses, but he pushed the impulse from
him . . ." (139). And, indeed, he seems finally to flee from Mrs.
Turner, as much because he fears her enticement as anything
else.

But when Gil Blount brings a new system with which to
seduce Cross, he also brings his wife Eva. Almost at once, upon
moving into the Blount apartment, before his desire for Eva
ever becomes apparent to him, Cross achieves a symbolic pene-
tration of her personality. The act is consummated with her
help; she invites him to enter the private studio where she keeps
her paintings; significantly, they are non-objective and therefore
of a highly personal nature: "He had the illusion, while studying
them, of standing somehow at the center of Eva's ego and being
captured by the private subjective world that was hers . . ."
(205). Immediately thereafter he is emboldened to rifle her stor-
age areas during her absence and read the diaries which he

finds. Whether or not he admits it to himself, at least part of his motivation for his murder of her husband that night must derive from Cross's revitalized sexual desire.

This motive for the murder is not really dissimilar to the one which Cross does admit. On the night he meets the Blounts, he observes the manner by which Blount and another Communist, Jack Hilton, humiliate and finally reduce Bob Hunter to a cringing wretch purely for their pleasure. After reflection, he decides that the ideals proposed by any collective, any institution, serve only to hide the real reason for man's participation in institutionalized activity. The will to power, he decides, is the principle that finally underlies all human activity. It follows that man wants all the power that he can get and that the greatest power would be the power to be as God, capable of continuing or concluding the life of others. Institutions may simply serve, therefore, as the loci for the transmission of power from superior to inferior, always with a sensual satisfaction resulting, usually for the superior: "Once a thorough system of sensual power as a way of life had gotten hold of a man's heart so that it ordered and defined all his relations, it was bound to codify and arrange all of his life's activities into one organic unity. This systematizing of the sensual impulses of man to be a god must needs be jealous of all rival systems of sensuality, even those found in poetry and music" (201).

Cross realizes, after observing the conscious application of power for pleasure by Blount and Hilton, that his own past is a series of unconscious attempts at sensual fulfillment. The way in which his realization clarifies his own muddled past is so overpowering that he feels he is under the spell of a vision: "This vision made reality more meaningful, made what his eyes saw take on coherence and depth. For the first time since that snowy evening in Chicago when he had decided to flee, when the waters of desire had drained off the world and had left it dry of interest, meaning began to trickle back again . . ." (201).

That night Cross has the opportunity to act in a godlike manner. As he observes Blount and Herndon struggling, he decides that he will discontinue life for both of them. They both profess belief in political systems in order to participate in sensual power; therefore they have no right to live and hurt such politically and psychologically naive people as Bob Hunter. Once he kills them, however, he realizes that in judging and executing them he had committed the same crime for which they were punished: "But, if he resented their being little gods, how could he do the same? His self-assurance ebbed, his pride waned under the impact of his own reflections. Oh. Christ, their disease had reached out and infected him too" (230). Ever since he left Chicago, he had felt himself struggling to escape a dreamlike existence. He had thought that his vision of the sensualization of power had restored clarity to his world. Now he realizes that his vision has not freed, but more deeply confined him: "He had acted, had shattered the dream that surrounded him, and now the world, including himself in it, had turned mockingly into a concrete, waking nightmare from which he could see no way of escaping. He had become what he had tried to destroy, had taken on the guise of the monster he had slain" (230-231).

Book IV begins with a quotation from *Macbeth:* The wine of life is drawn; and the mere lees/Is left this vault to brag of." This passage in which Macbeth despairs over the murder he has just committed was one of Kierkegaard's favorites; he quotes it once in *The Sickness Unto Death* and twice in *The Concept of Dread.* The context in which the quotation appears in *The Sickness Unto Death* is most helpful in understanding the moment at hand in *The Outsider.* Under the heading "Continuation of Sin," Kierkegaard is discussing "The Sin of Despairing over One's Sin":

> Despair over sin in an attempt to maintain oneself by sinking still deeper. As one who ascends in a balloon rises by casting weights from him, so does the despairing man sink by casting from him the good (for the weight of the good is uplift), he sinks, doubtless he thinks he is rising—he does indeed become lighter. Sin itself is the struggle of despair; but then when strength is exhausted there must needs be a new potentiation, a new demoniacal introversion, and this is despair over one's sin. This is a step in advance, as ascent in the demoniacal, but of course it means sinking deeper in sin. It is an

attempt to impart to sin as a positive power firmness and interest, by
the fact that now it is eternally decided that one will hear nothing
about repentance, nothing about grace. Nevertheless despair over
sin is conscious of its own emptiness, conscious of the fact that it has
nothing whatever to live on, not even a lofty conception of one's own
self. Psychologically it is a masterly line Macbeth utters after the
murder when he is in despair over his act (Act ii, Scene 3) . . . .[12]

Kierkegaard employs Macbeth's agonized cry when he is discussing despair; it is appropriate that Wright uses part of the
same speech as a motto and then entitles Book IV "Despair."
Further, the description of the despairer as a sinking man gives
added resonance to the choice of title for Book III, "Descent."
And the characterization of Cross as an atheist is given additional
credibility here, in that a state is described which Cross has
already reached: "In the main he accepted the kind of world that
the Bible claimed existed; but for the sufferings, terrors, acci-
dental births, and meaningless deaths of that world, he rejected
the Biblical prescriptions of repentance, prayer, faith, and
grace. He was persuaded that what started on this earth be
rounded off and somehow finished here" (143).

Kierkegaard also quotes the passage by Macbeth in *The Concept of Dread*, then amplifies by writing: "It is true Macbeth was
a murderer, and therefore in his mouth these words ring with a
note of truth which is terrible and harrowing, and yet everyone
who has lost inwardness can with good reason say, 'The wine of
life is drawn,' and can say too, 'There's nothing serious in mor-
tality, all is but toys'; for inwardness is precisely the fountain
which springeth up unto eternal life, and what issues from this
fountain is precisely seriousness."[13] "Inwardness is therefore
eternity, or the determinant of the eternal in a man."[14] "Some
deny the eternal in man. That very instant 'the wine of life is
drawn,' and every such individual is demoniacal."[15]

If one part of Cross is Adam the innocent, the other part of the
dialectic which is his being is Cross the demoniac. Just as *Adam*
is buried in *Damon*, so too is *Demon*. Late in his life, when his
crimes have been revealed, Cross is told by Ely Houston:

How magnificently you tossed away this God who plagues and helps man so much! But you did not and could not toss out of your heart that part of you from which the God notion had come. And what part of a man is that? It is desire. . . . Don't you know it? Why didn't you just live a quiet life like all other men? That's the correct way of being godless. Why be restless? Why let desire plague you? Why not conquer it too? (424).

Then Houston continues:

Desire? Why does man desire? It's crazy, for it's almost certain that he'll never get what he desires. . . . Isn't desire a kind of warning in man to let him know that he is limited? A danger signal of man to himself? Desire is the mad thing, the irrational thing. Damon, you peeled off layer after layer of illusion and make-believe and stripped yourself down to just simply naked desire and you thought that you had gotten hold of the core of reality. And, in a sense, you had. But what does one *do* with desire? Man desires ultimately to be a god. Man desires *everything*. . . . Why not? Desire is a restless, floating demon. . . . Desire tries to seize itself and never can. . . . It's an illusion, but the most solid one! Desire is what snared you, my boy. You felt that what obstructed desire could be killed; what annoyed, could be gotten rid of (425).[16]

This is an accurate assessment of Cross's activities after he succumbs to lawlessness. For he quickly learns that with the freedom he seizes in killing Joe Thomas and fleeing Chicago comes a compulsion to disregard the freedom of others. Very quickly too he learns to recognize others who have, like himself, rebelled against the conventional view of reality: "Cross could feel that Houston sensed the quality of the demoniacal in him, and he could feel the same in Houston" (134).

After his murder of Blount and Herndon, both of whom he has identified as exponents of lawlessness, he is forced to admit that he too has succumbed to the demoniacal. He is terrified when he learns that Ely Houston will conduct the investigation of the crime he has committed. But, while he recognizes Houston as his ultimate captor, he soon learns that he must confront a much more immediate danger. There is another Communist, Jack Hilton, who is also a demoniac, who professes Communism in order to exercise godlike powers, and Cross instinctively fears him: "To be in the power of a cold little god like Hilton was the most awful thing that could happen to a man" (259–260). This fear first manifests itself as unspecified hostility: "At some time in the future, he had a score to settle with this little god and it filled him with anger to think of it; then he was angry with himself for getting angry" (277). But though he knows that Hilton is a threat to him, Cross has an "irrational compulsion" (292) to see him. His feet take him to Hilton's hotel, and he slips into Hilton's room. With no particular object in mind, he pilfers the room while waiting for the absent Hilton; thus he learns that Hilton knows the truth about the murder of Herndon and Blount and has the evidence to use against him whenever he wishes. Cross tries to think of an alternative to yet another murder; he *wants* desperately to retrieve himself from the lawless road that he has taken.

As he waits for Hilton, Cross may think that he has not yet decided what his course of action will be. But when he turns on the radio and tunes in a program of jazz music (295), it is plain that lawlessness will prevail in Damon in this instance. Back when he had first come to New York and was in a kind of psychological hibernation at Mrs. Turner's, he had spent much of his time listening to the sound of jazz floating up from her quarters. A man damned to reflection, he came to realize the source of his attraction to jazz: "Blue-jazz was the scornful gesture of men turned ecstatic in their state of rejection; it was the musical language of the satisfiedly amoral, the boastings of the contentedly lawless, the recreations of the innocently criminal" (140). Later, in contemplating the systematizing of the sexual impulse by modern political theologies, "Cross . . . marveled at the astuteness of both Communist and Fascist politicians who had banned the demonic contagions of jazz" (200). Waiting for Hilton, then, Cross has already succumbed once again to the temptation to lawlessness. When Hilton comes, though Cross may argue with him, the issue is never in doubt. As he prepares to shoot Hilton, Cross has an eminently practical reason for turning up a "leaping flood of jazz music" (301), but the symbolism of the act is inescapable.

Once again the aftermath of surrender to lawlessness is revulsion: "he was deeper now than ever in the consequences flowing from his compulsive acts. He would be caught. . . . All right, so what? He was already lost anyway . . ." (305). Still, he is not the point of confession, and he seems to be revived by his successful denial of complicity in the murder of Hilton, first to the police and then to the Communists. Moreover, there is reason now for him to dare hope for some happiness in this world. He has found his Eve, his complementing part, in Eva, his sister in spirit, as Houston later calls her (421), and they share a short respite comforting one another. But Houston's pursuit is implacable, and when Cross is finally picked up, he is, in one way, relieved: "his despair drained off in one second and he felt that he wanted to sleep" (373).

Although he has been apprehended for questioning, Cross is not worried about the outcome. On the contrary, he seems to welcome the opportunity to stand before society and scorn its conventions, to play the role of Meursault. He is a free man, so he thinks, and wants the chance to proclaim it. Rather than allowing the representatives of society to question him, he has a grandiose question ready to ask them (376). But the interrogation does not realize his expectations. He is viewed not as the individual who has defied society and the universe, but as Cross Damon, who abandoned his family and indirectly caused the death of his mother. Indeed, he comes to fear that the only result of the interrogation will be his detention for psychiatric inspection—he who is the culmination of the history of rational men. He is able to maintain his facade, though, and Houston is forced to release him for lack of evidence.

The information that Lionel Lane is really Cross Damon is enough, however, to destroy Eva. Having trusted Cross completely, having by word and deed revealed the innermost parts of her self to him, she feels a crushing sense of betrayal when she is told of his tawdry reality. Now she can believe his confession of murder which she had previously rejected. Cross protests that while his actions have been demonic his heart has been innocent, but his attempts at exculpation gain no acceptance at all. Wildly Eva runs from his presence, to leap to her death.

The shock of Eva's death seems only to make Cross more resigned to his despair. He accepts responsibility for her death; it was his bad faith, his "falsely pledged promise" (407), that had prompted her act. For Sarah Hunter, Eva's friend, the death serves as an incentive; in response to the absurdity around her, she returns to the Church. From that vantage point, she can see Cross for what he is: "You are a *devil!* . . . You're making fun of me and it ain't *right*. It ain't *good* to laugh at people for things like that" (416). Although she may not know why Cross is a demon, she nevertheless reconizes that he is one.

The visitor who arrives within a few minutes knows why; when Ely Houston enters the room he justifies his reputation as a detective. For, having no clues that provide any exterior meaning for the three murders under investigation, he decides to look for interior meaning. So when he learns that the man known as Lionel Lane may be Cross Damon, he asks the Chicago police to search Damon's room and send him an inventory of its furnishings. The list of authors on that inventory suggests to him a definite kind of personality: "That was the first real clue. Your Nietzsche, your Hegel, your Jaspers, your Heidegger, your Husserl, your Kierkegaard, and your Dostoevski were the clues. . . . I said to myself that we were dealing with a man who had wallowed in guilty thought" (421). Apparently the common element in the thought of all these authors that Houston considers "guilty" is the acknowledgement of the role of the subjective in establishing the bounds of the real and the acceptable. For one charged with the responsibility of protecting the established beliefs, he could with conscious irony call such acknowledgements "guilty thought."

There is another author who could have been mentioned;

both Cross and Houston have read Sartre. For Houston's psychological description of Cross at this point derives heavily from *Being and Nothingness*. As I have earlier pointed out, Houston locates the source of all human action, including demonism, in desire. Further, he argues, "man desires ultimately to be a god!" (425) This argument comes close to Sartre's exact words (in translation): "To be a man means to reach toward being God. Or if you prefer, man fundamentally is the desire to be God."[17]

Cross has withstood a great deal; now he can withstand no more, and he breaks, to scream for the torture to end. In a sense, he seems to hope for arraignment and trial; conviction and punishment would at least suggest an order outside himself, even if inimical to him. But, to his consternation, Houston, wisely recognizing that he probably could not obtain a conviction, merely says: "*You're free!* Just like that" (429). As Houston views it, the real conflict has been and still is internal: "It's between *you* and *you*, you and yourself" (430). At this turn of events, Cross suffers what might be described as a Pascalian moment of recognition: "Always back deep in his mind, he had counted on their railing at him, storming, cursing, condemning, Instead, nothing, silence, the silence that roars like an indifferent cataract, the silence that reaches like a casual clap of thunder to the end of space and time . . ." (431).

Rather than serving as a protest against the whole of existence, Cross is forced to acknowledge that his efforts have been met by the silence of "an alien world looming implacably over and against him" (431). This acknowledgement is not, however, so pessimistic as it may at first seem. For if one finally is able to cast aside his foolish expectations of living, then one can begin at last to value sheer existence. Thus Cross comes to value Being itself and in doing so finds himself free of the demon of desire (431).[18] He chooses Being, makes a choice; Book V is therefore aptly entitled "Decision."[19]

With the disappearance of his urge to be as God, Cross can once again be as man and even begin to grope toward a relationship with God. He recognizes that one cannot survive alone, for alone one can find only nothing (439), and that "starting from scratch every time is . . . is no good" (439). This admission is a far cry from his earlier arrogance: "A man creates himself . . ." (51); it is more a Kierkegaardian acceptance of the necessity for the Self to be constituted by a Power: "Christianity has never subscribed to the notion that every particular individual is in an outward sense privileged to begin from scratch."[20] And if one does not start from scratch, one starts in that perplexing state of innocence/guilt that constitutes dread, the ambiguity of which lasts until one recognizes that "innocence is ignorance."[21]Thus in his dying breath Cross can maintain that he has been innocent (or ignorant) of his guilt, the guilt that he finally accepts, the guilt which confers upon him the true freedom, the freedom to seek atonement.

[1] "The Existential Darkness: Richard Wright's *The Outsider,*" *Wisconsin Studies in Contemporary Literature,* 1 (Fall 1960): 20.

[2] Richard Wright, *The Outsider* (New York: Harper and Row, 1965), 1. Hereafter, page references will be incorporated into the text.

[3] Translated, with an introduction and notes, by Walter Lowrie (Princeton: Princeton University Press, 1967), xii.

[4] *Ibid.,* 39.

[5] In *Being and Nothingness,* trans. and with an introduction by Hazel E. Barnes (New York: Philosophical Library, 1956), Jean-Paul Sartre writes, 47: "Others so as to make the Not a part of their very subjectivity, establish their human personality as a perpetual negation." This is an accurate description of Cross Damon.

[6] *The Concept of Dread,* 38.

[7] *Ibid.,* 47.

[8] *Ibid.,* 60.

[9] Translated, with an introduction and notes, by Walter Lowrie (Princeton: Princeton University Press, 1954), 148.

[10] *The Concept of Dread,* 100.

[11] *Ibid.,* 38

[12] *The Sickness Unto Death,* 241.

[13] *The Concept of Dread,* 130.

[14] *Ibid.,* 134.

[15] *Ibid.,* 135.

[16] At first in the novel "desire" seems only to indicate "sexual desire," but gradually it becomes sheer, unlocalized desire. *See Being and Nothingness,* 382–399, for Sartre's explanation of the relationship between sexual desire and sheer desire.

[17] *Ibid.,* 566.

[18] See *Being and Nothingness,* for a discussion of the acceptance of Being, 571–575.

[19] Widmer equates decision with death in his discussion of the title of Book V. I feel I must take issue with this equation, because, as far as I can see, the fact that Cross is killed by the avenging Communists has nothing to do with the fact that he has finally decided to accept the universe and himself as each exists.

[20] *The Concept of Dread*, 65.

[21] *Ibid.*, 37.

The Knife and the Saw
in *The Dollmaker*

*T*he opening scene of Harriette Arnow's *The Dollmaker* (1954)[1] could hardly be more expressive. On a rainy October afternoon in 1944, in the mountains of Kentucky, Gertie Nevels, sick child cradled in her arms, forces her reluctant mule off the familiar soft ground onto a highway. Her long thighs gripping his flanks, the large, plain woman subdues the mule's bucking, then makes him stand still on the center line before an approaching army sedan, which skids off the road when the driver maneuvers to avoid hitting them. When the enraged officer, being chauffeured from Oak Ridge on urgent business, gestures toward his pistol and orders her out of the way, Gertie replies that he must either take her and her sick child to the doctor or kill her in order to pass. She sets to work to free the automobile, taking out her knife to clear the underbrush beneath it and frantically pushing it as the enlisted driver accelerates the engine. Having pushed the car back onto the road, Gertie has to perform a tracheotomy on her choking son Amos, the sight of which causes the officer to faint. Making it possible for her son to breathe, she seeks a poplar switch from which she can fashion a pipe to insert in the incision she has made, incidentally slashing down from a tree a placard that recruits workers for Willow Run. There is, in cumulative effect, an allegorical confrontation: the toneless brigadier, representing abstract, distant, but terrible, indeed ultimate, mechanical power, is opposed by woman whose only power is the sheer will of her being.

Gertie's deft use of the knife prompts the general's admiration, but she dismisses her skill: "I've allus whittled" (22). "What?" he wants to know. Her behavior, as she replies, is revealing:

She looked down at the hand that held the poplar wood, the back brown and wrinkled, fingernails black and ragged, then at the palm, smooth with the look of yellowed leather. It was as if the hand were a page engraved with names while, she looking now at the poplar wood, repeated: 'Hoe handles, saw handles, ax handles, corn-knife handles, broom handles, plow handles, grubben-hoe handles, churn-dasher handles, hammer handles, all kinds of handles—it takes a heap of handles.' (22)

Gertie seems to understand that her knife is, in effect, an extension of her hand, the tool by which she imposes her existence upon her environment. Moreover, each specification of a handle that she carves describes yet another tool with which she can grasp her immediate world. The complex of tools that a human arranges around himself constitutes, for Martin Heidegger, in *Being and Time*, his primordial world. Rather than viewing a thing as merely something to analyze into its various qualities and thus dispersing that thing into distant space, one puts each thing where it belongs and creates a totality, a network, tightening up and drawing near one's place, one's world. The subject/object split that has caused so much alienation for modern man is thus obviated. Gertie has a very strong sense of being at home and a confidence that she can maintain the integrity of that home. Her world is, in Heidegger's phrase, "ready-to-hand." She talks to the plants and animals, her legs grip the mule, her hands reach out to change those things which need changing, even the diphtheria-swollen throat of her son.

The officer grants the utilitarian value of her skill, but, he demurs, "There wouldn't be much fun in handles" (23). He seems to sense the difference between work and play: one's work is dictated by the constraints of the external world, but one's fun, or play, results from the free expenditure of superabundant energy. Work concerns itself with what is actual, but play devotes itself to what is possible; work tires, but play, which may be every bit as strenuous, refreshes. Gertie understands the officer's distinction, for she replies that she has had little time "fer whittlen foolishness"—just a few dolls for her daughter Cassie. Perhaps because at that moment she realizes that even the dolls originated in a practical consideration—otherwise Cassie would have had no dolls—Gertie then admits to a sheer extravagance: ". . . I'm aimen to work up a piece of wild cherry wood I've got. It's big enough fer the head an shoulders uv a fair-sized man . . ."

That block of wood serves Gertie as a symbol of possibility. She seems to feel that as long as she possesses it as a project, gradually carving the figure that her vision discovers in it, she will be able to shape and fashion her total world. She understands, too, that the figure she brings out of the wood will be a self-assessment of her own intentions: she has thought of Jesus, of other Biblical characters, of Judas. The possibilities of human behavior range from the model of self-sacrifice provided by Jesus (though Gertie admits that she has never been able to see his face, his uniquely human aspect) to the model of betrayal provided by Judas (though Gertie certainly does not contemplate Judas before his sin, motivated by some obscure reason, but rather the remorseful Judas, just beginning to feel how far short he has fallen).

Gertie's abiding purpose, to preserve her family, is accomplished on that October afternoon, for she reaches the doctor's office, to place her son under his care. In a few days the family is reunited in its home and Gertie hopes that the rhythm of traditional life will resume. She is at pains to instruct her five children from the Bible and from her store of family history; Sunday is kept holy, and a visit to her parents' home honors them. But signs have already appeared that point to change. In the doctor's office Gertie had dropped her knife in surprise at a complex financial transaction: the officer had charitably tricked her into accepting forty dollars in change for the five dollar bill that she had tendered him in payment for the ride. Gertie had also felt so out of her element that she had deferred to the judgment of her husband Clovis, whose only claim to superior wisdom derives from his membership in the male sex. Further, Clovis has been directed by the draft board to report for his physical examina-

tion. All the other men in the locality have already been taken—
Gertie's only brother has been killed in action; one of Clovis'
brothers is missing in action—so that the approaching fragmentation of Gertie's nuclear family is merely the last skirmish in the
defeat of the community.

Making every exertion, Gertie tries to protect her family from
external threats. She is especially attentive to those of her children who most need her love. Reuben, his Biblical name indi-
cating his position as eldest son, is like his mother in being at
one with nature and ill at ease with people. Cassie, actually
"Keziah," a name announcing her position as second daughter, is
like her mother in needing an outlet for her innermost thoughts;
where Gertie has her block of wood, Cassie has her imaginary
playmate Callie Lou. Both mother and daughter recognize the
special nature of their bond: Gertie perceives her daughter's
fragility and habitually cuddles her and chafes her thin, delicate
legs; Cassie habitually fondles and playfully kicks the block of
wood and talks, much more than her siblings, about the figure in
it.

For all of her children Gertie has a single goal: she has the
Jeffersonian belief that spiritual independence arises from private property, so she has struggled throughout her fifteen-year
marriage to save enough money to buy even a very small farm.
She now has the required amount and a place picked out; she
seems desperate to get her family to a haven before a calamity
can strike. With Cassie, she walks over to the Tipton place,
whose appearance evokes a golden age, a homestead in Eden:

> Past the beehives and the orchard, sheltered by the curve of the
> ridge side, and on a southern slope where the early sun struck fully,
> lay the flattish bench of ungullied land that held the house and yard
> and barns and garden spot. She smiled on the shake-covered roof of
> the old log house; the white oak shakes, weathered to a soft gray
> brownness, must have been rived in the wrong time of the moon, for
> they had curled in places, and in some of the little cup-like hollows
> moss had grown. Now in the yellow sun the moss shone more gold
> than green, and over all the roof there was from the quickly melting
> frost a faint steam rising, so that the dark curled shakes, the spots of

moss, the great stone chimney, all seemed bathed in a golden halo and Cassie called that the house had golden windows. (53)

There is a brief interlude, an Indian summer of hope, when it looks as if Gertie will be able to move to the Tipton place, where ". . . she might live and be beholden to no man, not even Clovis" (139). She cleans the new house and wanders the woods, watching Reuben with approval: ". . . she saw him take his pocket knife and cut a little crooked cedar away from a straight one so that the straight one might grow" (59). During the day that Clovis has reported for his physical examination, Clytie, the elder daughter, attempts to relieve the family of its worry by saying that her father might be deferred to work in a war plant. From that possibility Gertie recoils in horror: "He'd be better off in the war than in one a them factories!" (97) For Gertie knows her man; before his departure, Clovis had joked, "Aw, Gert, you're jealous a machinery like it was another woman" (83); and his observation is apt, for if he should get the chance, he would go to Detroit and then inevitably she and the children would be forced to follow him. Such a move would destroy the family's connection to its place: the women do not come back to give birth to their children (126), and the continuity of generations is broken.

When, after a period of time, word comes from Clovis, it is the command that Gertie has dreaded. He has housing for the family in Detroit, where he is working. There is no real option for Gertie; she must act the dutiful wife, and if that role were not sufficient to dictate her behavior, her mother's nagging, concocted of guilt and sentimentality, would be enough of a force. So Gertie and her children journey north.

The trip on the train is for Gertie one long assault on her previous being, one long experience of severing, the image which now becomes predominate in the novel. Gertie is constantly ill at ease among the crowds; indeed Sartrean *en soi* invades her being: ". . . the air that was like a stinking rotten dough pushed up her nose and down her throat" (148). Her use of a knife, her method of self-reassurance, is misinterpreted as a threatening action (153). Immediately, in the Detroit terminal, she is reduced to stereotype: ". . . a woman's eyes under a red scarf glared at her, and a wide red mouth said, 'Hillbilly,' spitting the words as if they shaped a vile thing to be spewed out quickly" (156). Gertie will come to know the scarf as a *babushka*, as she will come to know exploitation by having others' words substituted for her own—the experience will weaken her, as it does here: she acts so uncharacteristic that her children wonder at her behavior (157). The family is separated, some children clinging, while others easily adapt to the new order of things: "Mom, can I go get me a coke?" (156)

The taxi trip to the development is, if anything, even more traumatic than the train trip. There is a savage wind, which carries a blinding snow. There is a succession of tunnels and bridges to emphasize the experience of radical change. Modern transportation dominates their progress. "The railroad tracks multiplied, and twice jangling bells and red lights winging in the wind held them still while long freight trains went by with more smoke rolling down and blotting out the world" (168). Soon after, an airplane lumbers over on take-off with a roar that frightens even the adaptive Enoch, his Biblical name establishing his "thirdness" in the family. As they arrive in the development of low, shed-like buildings, Gertie once again has her view blocked by a train that rushes past (170). Suddenly, when the train ends, a typical unit is seen: "There was on either side the door a little window; in front of one was a gray coal shed; in front of the other a telephone pole, and by it a gray short-armed cross" (170). Gertie must be struck by the possible meaning of that clothesline post, for as soon as she enters her new home she leans against the back of the door and stretches out her arms in the posture of crucifixion (171).

All is confusion. The rooms are so small and crowded that Gertie, a large woman, loses that fundamental sense of relation to her space and blunders against first one thing and then another. A novice at the use of a gas stove, she causes an explosion that singes her hair and must convince her that she has somehow been cast into the fiery pit, as one child throws water on her, while another laughs (173). Even her fingers betray her, as she fumbles at knobs. Certainly the family has not come to the land of milk and honey, for even the milk, which is pasteurized, tastes strange to them (181). Meanwhile, the children are introduced to the radio, which is, appropriately, touting junk food (184). At the same time, Gertie faces her first commercial transaction—an opportunity to buy her daily number from the coal and ice man (186). Through her mind runs a refrain: "As a bird that wandereth from her nest, so is a man that wandereth from his place" (214). There is a nagging feeling that she has forgotten something (189).

All that has been forgotten is compressed in the block of wood, which is to follow the family by express. Gertie would have had no time for it, anyway, occupied as she is with getting her children enrolled in school, learning to shop, accepting a teeming life in the alley (seen always through a broken pane in the storm window), where the children are always yelling and adults, cursing or crying. Adjustment, Gertie realizes, ultimately means the reduction of each individual to an identical mold: as she leaves the school in which she has placed her children, she notes that the sound issuing from that huge place is like that of the factories that she had passed to get there (208).

She does resume her whittling—on wood that Clovis identifies as scrap from a war plant. Her whittling is not a respite from her work, though, but an attempt to kill time: she realizes that she is no longer master of her own seasonal and diurnal time, but rather is ". . . bossed by the ticking voice" (210). She therefore cannot become engrossed; she is ". . . not able to forget the knife, herself, everything except the thing growing out of the wood, as she had used to be in stray moments of time back home" (209). By her awareness of her hands (formerly invisible in their activity) she reveals the alienation that she now suffers from her immediate world.

By the time her block of wood does come, Gertie has become known at the school and in the alley as a whittler. Moreover, she discovers that people are willing to pay for her carving, she discovers the urban way of assessing value: before, her whittling had given satisfaction because it had enabled her to create something which expanded her direct relationship with her world, whether the whittling was toy or tool; now her whittling is valuable because of its appeal to other people. Since they will pay for what she does, she begins to experience guilt whenever she does any whittling that is not to be validated by a cash transaction (289).

Thus she spends her time carving a cross for a neighbor's mother—for twenty dollars (270). Once a monetary value has been placed upon her activity, an economic process becomes inevitable: the production of as many units as possible in as short a time as possible. Clovis is the foremost exponent of this process, for he has been thoroughly indoctrinated into the ethos of time-and-motion, the piece-rate world. Thus he calculates the loss of quality in Gertie's cooking: "Twenty-five dollars, . . . You can't feed seven a us, all good big eaters, on twenty-five a week. That ain't four dollars a week apiece. Why Gertie, . . . that ain't much more'n fifty cents a day apiece" (270–271). When Gertie admits that she has been trying to save some small part of his wages, he angrily declares: "Cain't you git it into yer head that millions an millions a people that makes a heap more money than I'll ever make don't save? They buy everything on time" (271). Since the whole system is geared to time (and therefore quantity), it is only a matter of time before the suggestion is made that Gertie should manufacture her Christs on a cross with a jigsaw (318).

All the while, as Gertie watches her family succumb to the inducements to live by installments, so she loses her battle to keep the memory of Kentucky alive in the majority of her family, to be used as a standard against which to judge their new life. Clovis simply accepts the fact that he is a number at the plant and tries to reorganize the family upon the industrial model, "Nevels' Woodworking Plant," as Enoch wants to call it (477). Indeed, infatuated with the new rhetoric of hype, Enoch adds that "No. 1" should be put after the title, to make people think there is more than one plant; such behavior is consistent with his admiration for anyone who can take advantage of another (264, 349). Amos, the youngest child, cannot remember Gyp, the dog, for his mother, but he can distinguish between the roars of the different trains that shake their unit (259–260). Clytie, the older daughter, becomes captivated by the suggestive sighs of the radio soap operas (325), the real opiate of the people. Cassie and Reuben, on the other hand, remain so wedded to their Kentucky past that they cannot adjust to or cope with their new surroundings. A hint of Cassie's failure occurs on Christmas Day, when she cuts the dress off a store-bought doll to clothe a wooden doll that Gertie had carved for her back home (287). Reuben, who cannot become a round peg at school for a Mrs. Whittle, retreats into a solitary preoccupation with long lines of coal cars that bring "Kentucky Egg" to the plants (324–325). The family is sundered: those who adjust will become as indistinguishable as if they were fashioned from templates, like the other products of Detroit; those who do not adjust will flee or die.

The first child to break is Reuben. At the age of puberty, he would perhaps be suffering enough confusion about role, even if he were not in a new, hated environment. For he must now conclude that a deep special relationship no longer exists between his mother and himself. His disappointment and sense of betrayal are evident in a scene which takes place in the alley. There has been an argument between Reuben and his friends and the sons of Joseph Daly, the garbage truck worker who is reputed to have political connections. Daly begins to berate Reuben, but Gertie is cautioned by friends not to interfere; she watches helplessly, therefore, as Daly humiliates her son and his "hillbilly" crudities. Then she is forced to furious action, as she observes what no one else would note: "Only a city fool wouldn't know he was opening a knife" (312). She grabs Reuben's arm, restrains him, keeps his intention from being discovered, ultimately carries him indoors; from Reuben's point of view, his mother has betrayed him, preventing his acting as a Kentucky man would have acted, emphasized that he is still a child by physically dominating him. When, later, Gertie tries to reason with him ("You'll have to quit carren a knife, son. Detroit's differ'nt"), Reuben's reply establishes the unbridgeable gulf between them: "I've allus carried a knife, I ain't a quitten now. I ain't a maken myself over for Detroit. I ain't a standen a taken nobody's lies—like you done" (316–317). Then he slams the door as he goes out, symbolizing for his mother the barrier between them and foreshadowing his later behavior.

Reuben's troubles at school increase. There is a conference between Gertie and Mrs. Whittle, but no concurrence. Reuben must be taught to conform, Mrs. Whittle demands. But, rather, Reuben has reached that point of rebellion at which one performs an apparently trivial action purely because it flashes a symbolic statement: he cuts across a field to come home, rather than stay on the sidewalk under the direction of the safety patrol (336). Clytie is quick to report that Reuben has broken the rules and to prophesy that he will be reported. In the confrontation between Reuben and Clovis that follows, the father begins reasonably—and ends by slapping his son hard enough to draw blood (338). That blood signifies the hemorrhaging of the family. Ashamed, Clovis diverts his anger to Gertie: "His voice rose, drove in the knife, and turned it round and round. 'You know you never was no good at talken. You allus look like you wanta fight. That's part of his trouble'" (339). Later, Gertie tries to talk to her son in his bed, as her shadow is cast upon the wall by the light from a steel pour in the neighboring mill. Her inability to act as mother is accompanied by her observation of her silhouette: "She watched herself melt. One moment there was a thin shivering shadow, then nothing moved on the wall" (340). Cut off from her son, who runs away to Kentucky the next day, destined to become a backward hired hand on other people's land.

The pressures have steadily increased for six-year-old Cassie to meet society's norms. The most serious of her aberrancies is her continued reliance upon her imaginary playmate Callie Lou. Clovis, now always tired and testy from shift-work, admonishes Gertie: "You've got to make her quit them foolish runnen and talken-to-herself fits. The other youngens'ull git to thinken she's quair, and you'll have another Reuben" (367). He is prompted to think of Cassie's divergence as an example for a generalization that he has just made: "That's one a yer big troubles, Gert, . . . you won't give in to bein like other people. But it's somethen millions an millions a people has got to do, and the sooner a person learns it, the better" (366). Clovis customarily thinks in terms of millions now, as Gertie notices (368).

However much she may detest Detroit, Gertie tries to abide by Clovis' views. She will force Cassie to give up Callie Lou, even as she has given up Reuben. She will carve the cheap crosses and dolls in hateful labor for the money they command, even though she has lost her touch: ". . . the knife, as if remembering the old days when it worked as it willed, was slow and awkward, even contrary to the wood, so that the face seemed no face at all" (376). Ironically, her stubborn hand had just carved a club-footed doll, when Gertie calls Cassie, to order her to give up Callie Lou (379). Gertie wants to tell Cassie to keep the witch child, that everyone needs his private thing, but she distrusts her intuitions.

Thus Gertie forces Cassie out of her home into the alley, thinking that her daughter will no longer need the fantasy friend if she has some real playmates. Cassie learns, instead, to be secretive, to linger along the fence where she can continue to live with Callie Lou. It is only a matter of time until Cassie's retreat into fantasy extends beyond the bounds of safety. In searching for her one day, Gertie looks through the fence to see that Cassie has strayed onto the railroad tracks: "It was a narrow crack, but wide enough for her to see, with one eye against it, Cassie's red babushka on the other side, so close she could have touched it could her glance have been her hand" (403).

But the world she can see is no longer the world she can control—the roar of an airplane drowns out her cry of warning.

Frantically Gertie tries to find a hole in the fence, as horror freezes the movement of time. Now Gertie discovers the approach of the through train and, unable to outscream the airplane, desperately searches for something to throw as a warning. The *en-soi* has become viscous: "The swampy earth held no rock—nothing" (404). Bloody from trying to butt through the fence, Gertie staggers up to Cassie in time to see a lone boot, before other people try to lead her away. A neighbor appears, to help her try to stanch the flow of blood from the severed legs, but Cassie dies in her arms. Keziah was one of Job's rewards for his steadfastness, one of the children given to him after his tribulations. Gertie must doubt that she will be so blessed.

When Gertie is finally brought back to her unit, she is obsessed to work at her block of wood. Perhaps it is the deepest part of her being attempting to express its grief-work; perhaps it is the effort to assert some unquenchable belief in possibility, even after the loss of Reuben and Cassie—the two motives are not inconsistent. But as Gertie bends to carve, a train passes, and she drops her knife (415). Nor can she hold onto the knife, the next time she tries to carve (420). Her sense of wholeness has been destroyed: "Telephone poles, a row of chimneys, smoke and an airplane tore apart her sky" (430). Soon she is constantly under the influence of phenobarbitol, as she fumbles with the block and searches Scripture for solace. Though she had always before found some text that offered help, now she can only respond to Job's bitter protest (444): "For there is hope of a tree, if it be cut down, that it will sprout again, and that the tender branch thereof will not cease . . . But man dieth, and is laid low . . . and the river wasteth and drieth up: so man lieth down, and riseth not" (Job XIV, 7/12). Gertie does not seem to be inflating herself to liken her condition to that of Job's, for she too has tried to live in honor of God, yet is forced by Him to endure undeserved suffering.

Gradually, though, the weather begins to change and the ground to get warm. Spring is signaled for the children by the return of the popsicle truck, but for the adults more ancient

vernal activities occur. People clear out their accumulated winter trash; mothers have a desire to plant flowers, even though
every realistic consideration tells them that the neighbors' children will pull them up as soon as they break the ground. In that
great swarming area, the inhabitants even strive for privacy by
erecting fences. During that communal effort, Gertie even feels
a sense of returning to her former, ready-to-hand world: "She
took the hammer; the feel of it, the same old hammer she had
used back home, was good in her hand" (453).

In time the war in the Pacific is concluded by the explosion of
the atomic bombs. There is a Japanese family in a neighboring
unit, the mother of which is comforted by the other women
when she cries for her race. They do not realize that the bomb is
merely the ultimate achievement of the industrial process that
controls them—they can only feel her human agony. Indeed,
when they do grasp the larger consequences of the end of the
war, they are concerned: ". . . it was as if the people had lived on
blood, and now that the bleeding was ended, they were worried
about their future food" (495).

The natural activities that reawaken Gertie's interest in her
existence do not, therefore, comfort Clovis. For his life is con-
trolled by economic phenomena so abstract that he cannot identify them; with the conclusion of the war, labor-management
strife intensifies, and Clovis, looking for the enemy, sees only
other pawns as the objects of his hatred. In a fight with some
men hired to harm a fellow worker, Clovis is injured so visibly
that he dare not report for work. So he hides at home, nursing
his desire for revenge. The night comes when he steals Gertie's
knife, to use in his attack upon the young man who had assaulted
him. Gertie will not allow herself to believe the evidence that
Clovis has killed his attacker, that blood from the knife stains the
water in which she places it (568). But the act is revealed by the
sand on his shoes, so that, like Cain's murder of Abel, "the blood
crieth . . . from the ground" (Genesis, III, 10). Still, she dare not
admit the truth to herself.

The fears of the people in the alley are well founded, for layoffs and strikes begin almost immediately. Clovis, out on strike, is rendered useless. Searching for odd jobs, he finds that expenses absorb almost all that he makes. He discovers, too, that all the promises of instant credit that sweeten the air of American society do not apply to the unemployed. Gertie, disgusted at the spectacle that she must become, tries to peddle the jigsawed dolls through the alleys and hangs a sign announcing that she will take in washing and ironing. But all of her neighbors are equally poor. There is democracy in the alley, for the ethnic slurs seem to decrease, as the children learn the economic slurs necessary for the game of "strike": "Scab, Scab. You've crossed a pickut line!" (579)

There are times when there is absolutely nothing to do— meals are easy to prepare when they consist of spaghetti smothered with a can of tomato soup. Gertie has time to work on her block of wood, then. But the presence in the wood seems only to precipitate her own repressed feelings of guilt, for she becomes so remorseful about the murder that the knife drops to the floor: "I stood still for it—I kept—I could ha spoke up" (584). She is forced to admit that the figure resembles Judas, the Judas whose ineffectual return of the money could never return the life that it bought.

It is at that moment that an order for dolls is placed by a former neighbor, Mrs. Anderson, whose husband has discovered a way to be useful to plant management. Now all Mrs. Anderson has to do is dose herself with enough phenobarbitol to keep from gagging on her new life (588). The woman has even brought an advance of $50, to be used to purchase the necessary wood. Gertie stares at the money in her hand, her mind surely wondering if that formerly trusty agent, her hand, is going to commit a betrayal, Clovis wants to take Gertie to an art supply store, to get the proper seasoned wood, "walnut or cherry or dogwood or holly" (590), the woman had specified. But Gertie, true to her thrify nature, wants to go first to the scrapwood shop at which she has gotten wood in the past. Perhaps she can purchase an adequate wood there and save some of the $50 for family use. Such a consideration for scrimping on the quality of a thing is, of course, a far cry from the old Gertie.

The final scene of the novel matches the novel's initial scene in its allegorical intensity. As Gertie leaves the unit, the eternal tinkerer, Clovis, is excited about using his jigsaw to fashion the dolls, instancing a pig as one of the patterns: ". . . you make real good pigs . . ." (581). Hardly needed to be compared with that emblem of selfishness, Gertie makes her way along, trying to sell dolls as she goes. First she meets a woman who tells her that she is lucky to have a means of making at least a little money (592). Then she observes a family which has been evicted, to which she makes a contribution, passing up the bills in her pocket, but salving her conscience by donating a quarter, instead of a dime (593). The family, it turns out, Gertie has known; the mother has wanted to see Gertie, to give her a cactus. The plant is older than her children, the woman says: it is clearly a prized possession, but the woman gives it away to assure that at least it will receive good treatment. The furniture and the children of the family are scattered through the alley.

Gertie is quick to accept the plant, before any more of the woman's tears fall on it to scald it. Then she delightedly hurries home ". . . with the pot, large and wrapped in silver foil, held carefully in both hands . . ." (594), before remembering her interrupted mission and reflecting upon her present behavior. Back at the time of Cassie's death, Gertie had worked on her figure, drawing out the hand which seems to be giving something back, a gesture which prompted her to think of Biblical examples of such behavior: "Who gave and what gift, she wondered? Jonah with a withered leaf from the gourd vine—Esau his birthright—Lot's wife looking at some little pretty piece of house plunder she could not carry with her—Job listening to the words of Bildad and wondering what next the Lord would want?" (444). At the time, Gertie's thoughts had skipped all of the examples to seize upon Job's protest: plants may survive, but what of man? Now, though, she seems to perceive that all of her examples are compressed into the figure of her destitute neighbor, who has had her American birthright of at least a minimal economic security taken from her, who must relinquish her "house plunder," who must give up even the "gourd vine," which, like Gertie's block, focused her sense of being. Gertie is shaken, for she must see that for the woman the plant has survived, while the family has died. Clovis notices her inwardness: "Gert, you look—funny—kinda pale. You don't want to be gitten sick again—not now" (594). She assures him that she is all right, but she continues to sit next to the block of wood, clearly distracted, not daring to wonder "what next the Lord would want."

But she knows what she must demand of herself, even as she is presented with a temptation to ignore that stern inner summons. Clovis has an opportunity for a few days' work, repaairing machinery and clearing an old apple orchard. These wages might tide them over. There is even an added personal appeal: Gertie might receive some good apple wood for whittling. Unlike Eve, Gertie knows that she must not reach for the apple, but rather is now resolved to her future.

In preparation for her ultimate action, Gertie practices sacrifice, by going without supper and thus supplementing the scanty fare shared by Clovis and the children. Impatiently, she waits for her family to go to bed, so that she can work on her figure, combs out her unbobbed hair, and occasionally touches "the head, the hands, the cloth about the shoulders" (596). She seems to be reenacting the actions of the woman in Luke, VII, 38, who acknowledges her repentence by taking down her hair to use as a drying cloth for the feet of Jesus.[2]

Then Gertie is ready to act in imitation of Jesus. She places the block of wood in Amos' wagon, to begin her journey to the wood lot. Along the way, the procession attracts all the little children of the alley. Gertie must have known on that first day in Detroit, when she had stood in the attitude of the cross, that her life would come to this extremity. As she bears her cross, the children speculate upon the identity of the figure, making different guesses, but all clearly delighted by the ambiguity that encourages their individual perceptions. The owner of the lot settles upon an identity at once: "Christ?" (598) After a lengthy pause, Gertie replies, "Cherry wood," seeming to scourge herself by using the description that a materialistic society would understand, but in reality proudly asserting that she intends to craft her work from the best material available: "I want him—it—sawed into boards for whittling."

The anticipation of the screaming saw ripping into the block of wood no doubt leaves a lingering image in the minds of many readers. They could be tempted to understand the novel as a naturalistic lament about the destruction of the traditional rural values by the necessary evil of modern technology. Poor, naive, even ignorant Gertie passively awaits her doom in a world in which history has passed her by. But such a reading would be an imposition on the text, for the final tableau is not on the whirling saw, but upon a majestic woman, whose consciousness is beautiful and powerful because of its indebtedness to Biblical imagery, as she stands there, ax in hand, decision made, every bit as forceful as any pioneer who cleared the forests that became the dark fields of the republic.

The man says that the block is so large that his saw cannot handle it, that it will first have to be split by an ax. Through an enormous act of will, Gertie has brought to its end the block which has represented her life, and now, with a magnificent use of her hands, she, in effect, picks up the knife that she has dropped so often, she swings the ax to sacrifice herself for her children's future. No wonder that the alley children give a great shout when the block is sundered—it was done for them. A long time has passed and a great distance has been traveled since Gertie used her knife so effectively upon her world on the misty Kentucky road—she has had to learn, like Job, that life at its fullest is suffering—but her action here proclaims that she will submit to nothing but herself.

---

[1] (New York: Avon Books, 1974). Page references will be incorporated into the text.

[2] W. Ewing so interprets the woman's actions in Luke, in *Dictionary of the Bible*, ed. James Hastings, Rev. Frederick C. Grant and H. H. Rowley (New York: Charles Scribner's Sons, 1963), 359.

Cass Kinsolving:
Kierkegaardian Man of Despair

After the publication of William Styron's *Set This House on Fire* (1960),[1] several critics mentioned its existential element. Robert Gorham Davis wrote that it was "more or less existentialist,"[2] and David L. Stevenson placed it "in an existential world."[3] John Howard Lawson wrote that its "existentialist frame of reference is more pervasive than the psychological element in *Lie Down in Darkness*; . . ."[4] And Ihab Hassan noted that it "reminds us that existential fiction has become as indigenous to American as it is to Europe."[5] These generalizations do not, however, provide an adequate account of Styron's existential theme.

Only when Cass Kinsolving, the protagonist, is viewed as a Kierkegaardian man of despair does his life take on enough significance to justify its very full presentation. For although he seems unaware of it, Kinsolving's descriptions of his thoughts and actions during his exile in Europe are couched in Kierkegaardian terms. The introduction of the theme of despair into the novel is Kinsolving's exploration of his spiritual life in Paris. At that time, after having driven his family from him, he encounters a tart he knows, who tells him, "*Cass, tu es malade!*" And though he had denied his sickness then, Kinsolving, back in the United States several years later, admits the truth of the girl's observation, when he tells Peter Leverett:

> And the thing was, you see, I *was* sick. . . . What I was really sick from was from despair and self-loathing and greed and selfish and spite. I was sick with a paralysis of the soul, and with self, and with flabbiness. . . . I was very nearly sick unto death, and I guess my sickness, if you really want to know, was the sickness of deprivation, and the deprivation was my own doing, because though I didn't know it then I had deprived myself of all belief in the good in myself. The good which is very close to God. (269–270)

Though Cass has apparently never read Kierkegaard, Styron surely has: "despair," "self-loathing," "selfishness," "self," "sick unto death"—all suggest that Styron is positing Kinsolving as a character who travels through the stages of despair until he reaches the faith that saves him from madness. Styron relies mainly, of course, upon Kierkegaard's *The Sickness Unto Death.*[6]

The sickness unto death is, says Kierkegaard, despair (*SUD*, 7). This sickness can be regarded in two ways: (1) "Despair regarded in such a way that one does not reflect whether it is conscious or not so that one reflects only upon the factors of the synthesis" (*SUD*, 7); (2) "Despair viewed under the aspect of Consciousness" (*SUD*, 8). There are two forms of "Despair viewed under the aspect of Consciousness": (a) "Despair which is Unconscious that it is Despair," and (b) "Despair which is Conscious of being Despair" (*SUD*, 8). Of "Despair which is Conscious of being Despair," there are two forms: (1) "In despair at not willing to be oneself," and (2) "The despair of willing desparingly to be oneself" (*SUD*, 8). Each form of despair viewed under the aspect of consciousness can be seen in succession in Kinsolving as he searches Europe for spiritual peace.

The most vivid action in *Set This House on Fire* is the conflict between Mason Flagg and Cass Kinsolving, which is eventually resolved through the murder of Flagg by Kinsolving. But the motive force for the novel does not result from this conflict; Cass intrigues the reader not because he wars against Flagg, but because he wars against himself. And he knows that the source of his difficulties was not Flagg. As he emphatically tells Leverett some years after Flagg's murder, "It didn't *start* with Mason, I'm telling you, . . . It started in me, early, way back. . . . But it really started in Paris the year before, when I was sick and these here nightmares began to come upon me. It began *then*, . . ." (249)

And in his loquacious, half-erudite, half-illiterate speech, Cass begins to characterize his condition in Paris. He had been drunk, sexually unfaithful, unable to paint. "You know, you can't work without faith, and, boy, I was as faithless as an alleycat," he says (250). He is interpreting, however, an event which had occurred years before, had he known then that his salvation lay in faith, he might have avoided the inhuman punishment that he later gave himself. But only after he has murdered Flagg and has been given his freedom by Luigi Migliori, the philosophical Italian policeman, does Cass gain faith, the only Kierkegaardian antidote to despair (*SUD*, 216). The element of retrospection also invalidates another comment about his Paris condition that Cass later makes: "Boy, Kinsolving pitted against Kinsolving, . ." (250). This statement implies that Cass knew at the time that his condition resulted from his self being in conflict with itself; his comments immediately afterward show that he had not known the cause of his condition.

For as he admits, he had "had no such notions or insights there in Paris" (254). That he is aware as he talks to Leverett of what his trouble was in Paris is clear, though, by the redundancy of his references to his self for a few pages (254–255). But at the time, Cass had not known the cause of his condition. He had been so tied up in himself that he could not analyze himself.

On that day in Paris, having driven his family from him, Cass drunkenly wanders around the apartment, his steps carrying him to a window overlooking the city. He tells Leverett later,

> Well, I stood there for a long while. . . . And then finally, in a sort of doze, and with all my hatred and poison lost for the moment, or forgotten, I looked up. And I'll swear at the moment as I looked up it was as if I were gazing into the kingdom of heaven. I don't know quite how to describe it—this *bone-breaking* moment of loveliness. . . . Ah my God, how can I describe it! It wasn't just the *scene*, you see—it was the sense, the bleeding *essence* of the thing. It was as if I had been given for an instant the capacity to understand not just beauty itself by its outward signs, but the other—the *elseness* in beauty, this continuity of beauty in the scheme of all life which triumphs even to the point of taking in sordidness and shabbiness and ugliness, which goes on and on and on, and of which this was only a moment, I guess, divinely crystallized. . . . What was it, really? I just don't know—the weakness, the light-headedness, the booze, the vertigo. Yet it was there, and for the first time—the first moment of reality I think I had ever known. And the strange thing

was that it was in the midst of this, in the midst of a time when I was most wrapped up in self and squalor and meanness, I had a presentiment of selflessness: . . . It was no longer a street that I was watching; the street was inside my very flesh and bones, you see, and for a moment I was released from my own self, embracing all that was within the street and partaking of all that happened there in time gone by, and now, a.ıd time to come. And it filled me with the craziest sort of joy . . . (256–257)

According to the forms of despair that Kierkegaard views under the aspect of consciousness, Cass is starting to move from unconscious despair to despair conscious of its existence. His vision marks him as a Kierkegaardian *immediate* man:

The *immediate* man . . . is merely soulishly determined, his self or he himself is something included along with 'the other' in the compass of the temporal and the worldly, and it has only an illusory appearance of possessing in it something eternal. Thus the self coheres immediately with 'the other, . . .'

Now then there *happens*, befalls (falls upon) this immediate self something which brings it to despair; in no other way can this come about, since the self has no reflection in itself, that which brings it to despair is merely passive. That wherein immediacy has its being, or (supposing that after all it has a little bit of reflection in itself) that part thereof to which it especially clings, a man is deprived of by 'a stroke of fate,' in short, he becomes, as he calls it, unfortunate, that is, the immediacy in him receives such a shock that it cannot recover itself—he despairs. Or . . . this despair of immediacy occurs through what the immediate man calls an all-too-great fortune; . . (*SUD*, 80–81).

Uneducated though he is, Kinsolving discusses his experience by using Kierkegaardian images: e.g., Cass's "elseness" is Kierkegaard's "the other." When Cass discusses the vision, he suggests that liquor was responsible. The truth, though, was that he had gazed into "the kingdom of heaven," that he had established a God-relationship, and "the God-relationship infinitizes; but this may so carry a man away that it becomes an inebriation, . ." (*SUD*, 48). Or again, Kinsolving says that the vision was the result of vertigo, using a Kierkegaardian analogy to despair (*SUD*, 19, 22). While he is still in unconscious despair, the vision has "happened" that propels him into conscious despair.

After Cass has his vision, he passes out. Later he tells Leverett, "I can't say how long this moment of *rapture*—I guess, that's what is was—I don't know how long it lasted, maybe not more than half a minute, . . . Then a strange thing happened. . . . I fainted, blacked out" (258). His sense of immediacy has been shattered by a vision of eternity, and his self reacts as Kierkegaard predicts: ". . . this is the only way immediacy knows how to fight, the one thing it knows how to do: to despair and swoon—and yet it knows what despair is less than anything else. It despairs and swoons, and thereupon it lies quite still as if it were dead, . ." (*SUD*, 82).

There occurs then in Cass's recital the curious story of his youthful seduction of Vernelle Satterfield, which Styron slyly calls a "diversion" (259). Midway in it, though, Styron has Cass attach significance to the story:

> Maybe I seem to be getting away from the point. But you see, it was this girl and this moment in time which were so important to me that day in Paris, and I'll tell you about it. But I've often thought that it was not the girl so much—maybe because, whatever it was, it wasn't love—who was important to me, but the moment, the mood, the sad nostalgic glamour—call it what you will: the crystallization of a moment in time past which encompasses and explains and justifies time itself. (261–262)

The seduction takes on importance when Cass says that the mood surrounding Vernelle began to pervade his mind in Paris after his swoon; the mood came over him with a "heart-stopping and heart-rending immediacy" (266), until, as Cass says, "the joy was on me, the joy and the calm. It was a real euphoria" (267). Kierkegaard knows that happiness—and its peril:

> Even that which, humanly speaking, is the most beautiful and lovable thing of all, a feminine youthfulness which is sheer peace and harmony and joy—even that is despair. For this indeed is happiness, but happiness is not a characteristic of the spirit, and in the remote depths, in the most inward parts, in the hidden recesses of happiness, there dwells also the anxious dread which is despair; it would be only too glad to be allowed to remain therein, for the

dearest and most attractive dwelling-place of despair is in the very heart of immediate happiness. All immediacy, in spite of its illusory peace and tranquillity, is dread, and hence, quite consistently, it is dread of nothing; one cannot make immediacy so anxious by the most horrifying description of the most dreadful something, as by a crafty apparently casual half word about an unknown peril which is thrown out with the surely calculated aim of reflection; yea, one can put immediacy most in dread by slyly imputing to it knowledge of the matter referred to. For immediacy doubtless does not know; but never does reflection catch its prey so surely as when it makes its snare of nothing, and never is reflection so thoroughly itself as when it is . . . nothing. There is need of an eminent reflection, or rather of a great faith, to support a reflection based upon nothing, i.e. an infinite reflection. So even the most beautiful youthfulness which is sheer peace and harmony and joy, is nevertheless despair, is happiness. (*SUD*, 37–38)

In the years since his Paris vision, Cass has learned well the dialectical, happiness-despair quality of immediacy. The mood induced by his memory of Vernelle he had thought then to be "a real euphoria," but then he adds, "And, God, how stupid I was not to realize that the whole thing was a fraud!" (267)

In the state of immediacy, of false happiness that is really despair, of "joy, serenity, the calm," (267) Cass leaves the apartment for the Luxembourg Gardens, thinking he will be able to paint for the first time in months. At this time the passage previously quoted occurs, in which Cass is told, "*Cass, tu es malade!*" In such a state of false happiness, Cass resents what he considers an intrusion into his personal life: "No Montparnasse tart—especially one who had confronted me as if she were my own guilt made incarnate—was going to spoil my balmy day, see? So I suppose I said something rude, . . ." (269) Kierkegaard knows, also, the angry reaction to a suggestion that immediacy is false: "So when a man is supposed to be happy, he imagines that he is happy (whereas viewed in the light of the truth he is unhappy), and in this case he is generally very far from wishing to be torn from that illusion. On the contrary, he becomes furious, . ." (*SUD*, 66). But, no matter how hard Cass tries, he cannot recapture immediacy; by the time he reaches the Gardens, he later says, ". . . I was feeling *bad*. . . . And to top it all, worse than this was the anxiety I'd begun to feel—this dread, this fear that something bad was about to happen" (270). This is the Kierkegaardian "dread of nothing"; Cass only knows that "something bad was about to happen." Unable to stand his anxiety, Cass runs for home in a panic, there to throw himself on the bed, trying to protect himself by "lying dead." He sleeps, but a dream terrifies him into wakefulness.

In the dream Cass is being taken to the North Carolina state prison by his uncle, and he says later of his dream feelings,

> . . . I can remember the feeling of despair I had, because for the life of me I couldn't figure out what my crime was, or anything about it, other than that I had done something unspeakably wicked—surpassing rape or murder or kidnapping or treason, some nameless and enormous crime—and that I had been sentenced not to death or to life imprisonment but to this indefinite term which might be several hours or might be decades. Or centuries. (272–273)

Before his dream Cass was still in a state of despairing over the earthly. But his dream reveals that he is progressing into the next stage of despair: "Despair over the earthly or over something earthly is really despair also about the eternal and over oneself, in so far as it is despair, for this is the formula for all despair" (*SUD*, 97). As the dream continues, Cass, so he tells Leverett, is led to the lethal chamber:

> . . . then I woke up beneath the blanket half-smothered and howling bloody murder with the vision in my brain of the dream's last Christ-awful horror: which was my uncle, my kindly good old bald-headed uncle who'd reared me like a daddy, standing with a crucible of cyanide at the chamber door, grinning with the slack-lipped grin of Lucifer hisself and black as a crow in his round tight-fitting executioner's shroud. . . . (274)

At this point Styron is again relying upon Kierkegaard for imagery. The dream reveals Cass's unconscious awareness of his despair over the eternal, but it reveals also his conscience at work. He is guilty, of what he does not know, but he is being executed by his foster father, a God symbol. It is the method of execution that suggests a Kierkegaardian image: "A man seated in a glass case is not put to such embarrassment as is a man in his transparency before God. This is the factor of conscience" (*SUD*, 203).

Cass is thoroughly conscious now of despair, but contrary to what might be expected, his recognition is the first step toward his regeneration. As Kierkegaard says, unconsciousness "may be the most dangerous form of despair. By unconsciousness the despairing man is in a way secured . . . against becoming aware—that is, he is securely in the power of despair" (*SUD*, 69–70). Almost everyone suffers from one of two kinds of despair; if one is not unconscious of despair, then one must be conscious of it. This is Cass's new state. But consciousness of despair can take either of two forms: "despair at not willing to be itself; or . . . despair at willing to be itself" (*SUD*, 74). With his recognition of despair, Cass wills not to be himself.

When he first awakens, he thinks of suicide: "Then for the first time in my life, I guess, I honestly, passionately yearned to die . . ." (274). He does not kill himself, though, because of the dream:

> . . . I think I would have willingly done myself in in an instant if it hadn't been that the same dream which pushed me toward the edge also pulled me back in a sudden gasp of crazy, stark, riven torture: there wouldn't be any oblivion in death, I knew, but only some eternal penitentiary where I'd tramp endlessly up gray steel ladderways and by my brother-felons be taunted with my own unnameable crime and where at the end there would be waiting the crucible of cyanide and the stink of peach blossoms and the strangled gasp for life and then the delivery, not into merciful darkness, but into a hot room at night, with the blinds drawn down, where I would stand again, as now, in mortal fear and trembling. And so on in endless cycles, like a barbershop mirror reflecting the countless faces of my own guilt, straight into infinity. (274–275)

Cass's soul is at this point still within a Christian frame of reference:

. . . humanly speaking, death is the last thing of all; and humanly speaking, there is hope only so long as there is life. But Christianly understood death is by no means the last thing of all, hence it is only a little event within that which is all, an eternal life; . . . (*SUD*, 12)

Still, Cass plans to kill himself and his family when they return, so he lies in wait for them. While waiting, he dreams again, this time of immediacy:

And I saw some southern land with olive trees and orange blossoms, and girls with merry black eyes, and parasols, and the blue shining water. . . . there seemed to be a carnival or a fair: I heard the strumming music of a carrousel, which wound through it all like a single thread of rapture, and I heard a liquid babble of tongues and I saw white teeth flashing in laughter and, Lord love me, I could even smell it—this smell of perfume and pines and orange blossoms and girls, all mixed up in one sweet blissful fragrance of peace and repose and joy. (276)

Part of the dream comes from the memories of past happy experiences, but the most important part is "one sweet blissful fragrance of peace and repose and joy." Here Cass uses almost verbatim Kierkegaard's characterization of immediacy: "Even that which, humanly speaking, is the most beautiful and lovable thing of all, a feminine youthfulness which is sheer peace and harmony and joy—even that is despair" (*SUD*, 37). Although Cass has despaired, he still thinks he can substitute immediacy for faith, the only answer to despair (*SUD*, 77).

The next morning the delusion that he can regain immediacy forces Cass to forget his plans for murder and suicide. Beset by his guilt, he welcomes his family, embracing his wife and thinking, as he tells Leverett, ". . . of the day before, and the long night, and even Vernelle Satterfield and what she said about the divine spirit, which had indeed flowed right on out of me, and which to save my very life I knew I had to recapture" (278). The seduction of Vernelle has become symbolic: he had become so excited that he had been unable to perform the sexual act, and she had said, "Why, you *pore silly*. . . . Why the divine spirit just flowed right on out of you" (265). The flowing-out of the divine spirit, falling into despair, has its counterpart image in Kierkegaard: "Whence then comes despair? From the relation wherein the synthesis relates itself to itself, in that God who made man a relationship lets this go as it were out of His hand, . ." (*SUD*, 22).

After his dream of immediacy, Cass tries to force his consciousness of despair from his mind. Going to a doctor, he embarks upon a "regime which he was later to call his period of 'dull reasonableness'" (280). Kierkegaard knows, too, the attempts of the "immediate" man to regain immediacy, after having despair befall him:

> Meanwhile time passes. If outward help comes, then life returns to the despairer, he begins where he left off; he had no self, and a self he did not become, but he continues to live on with only the quality of immediacy. If outward help does not come, then in real life something else commonly occurs. (*SUD*, 83)

Cass fears the recurrence of his despair, but it comes, the result of an unpleasant incident with an American tourist couple (forerunners of the McCabes in Rome, when he has another attack). The memory of "the blue southern waters, the carrousel, the laughing girls—vaulted into his consciousness, no longer just a promise and a hope, but a command, rather, and an exhortation" (282), and he knows that he must seek his vision of immediacy in the south.

The Kinsolvings leave Paris for the south, where Cass hopes to find his vision. En route, the children contract scarlet fever, and it seems a miracle that they survive. They do, though, and the family settles in Toulon to recuperate. Here Styron first presents the solution to Cass's despair. When Cass talks to his Catholic wife about his fear that the children would die, she says that she had known that they would get well. And Cass, so he writes in his journal, had said:

> How did she know. And she said—why I had FAITH, thats all silly. And then I blew my top—saying something on the order of Faith my ass, it was a man named Alexander Fleming who did it you idiot, and penicillin & 75,000 francs worth of medical care product not of faith

in some dis-embodied gaseous vertebrate, and an hermaphrodite triply-damned incestuous one at that, but of mans own faith vain perhaps, but nonetheless faith in his hardwon decency & perfecta-bility & his own compassionate concern with his mortal, agonizing plight on a half burnt out cinder that he didn't ask to be set down on in the first place. . . . Then she said again quite firmly & finally: I had faith. (294–295)

Poppy knows that "the believer possesses the eternally certain antidote to despair, viz. possibility; for with God all things are possible every instant. This is the sound health of faith . . ." (*SUD*, 61). But Cass still rejects faith.

In conscious despair, his first impulse had been to commit suicide, in despair to will not to be himself. At Toulon he articu-lates for the first time his death-wish, mentioned earlier in the novel (55, 118, 195, 196, 238) but not earlier chronologically; he writes in his journal, "At least I understand the quality & quan-tity of what I do possess which is a mysterious self-hatred . . ." (293). He hates his weakness, as Kierkegaard predicts that a despairer should: "Just as a father disinherits a son, so the self is not willing to recognize itself after it has been so weak. In its despair it cannot forget this weakness, it hates itself in a way, . ." (*SUD*, 100).

In his state, Cass can find no peace, so the Kinsolvings move to Florence, then to Rome. Again Cass tries to "live on only with . . . immediacy" (*SUD*, 83). "The world of taste and sight and sound—all the sweet sensations Nature granted to the most uncomplicated mortal—were his once more; the air dripped sunlight, his nostrils quivered to long-forgotten odors, he felt he might live to a ripe old age" (296). Cass is still the "immediate" man: "He now acquires some little understanding of life, he learns to imitate the other men, noting how they manage to live, and so he too lives after a sort" (*SUD*, 83). The card game with the McCabes ends Cass's attempts to live the conventional life. At its cataclysmic conclusion, he rushes out into the life that he had abandoned in Paris.

Again filled with despair, Cass had drunkenly picked up a

whore. Though he does not know the reason for his actions, Kierkegaard does: the despairer "will seek forgetfulness in sensuality, perhaps in debauchery, in desperation he wants to return to immediacy, . ." (*SUD*, 105). When he had become conscious, Cass found himself lying naked in a filthy hotel room.

> For long perplexing minutes he grappled with the question of how came he there, and when, and why; there was a terrifying instant when he could not recall his own name. . . . All identity had fled him and he lay there quietly breathing—. . . After a time, by the slowest of stages, he regained his bearings; memory and reality came slipping back, as did his name, which he spelled out slowly to himself— K-i-n-s—. . . .(309)

He is still the "immediate" man, for "the immediate man does not recognize his self, he recognizes himself only by his dress, he recognizes. . . he recognizes that he has a self only by externals" (*SUD*, 84).

Here again Cass has the vision of "whirling carrousels and orange blossoms and the black eyes of girls" (311) that symbolizes immediacy to him. And here too Cass moves into a further stage of despair. He had been in despair at not willing to be himself; still Christianly oriented, he had despairingly thought of suicide, but fearing no end of his despair in death, he had attempted to keep his self drugged by immediacy or inebriation. Now he wills desparingly to be himself; he is defiant about his condition. As he sprawls on the vermin-infested bed, he screams, "*Dio non esiste!*" and, again, "*Non c'è Dio!*" (311) These screams mark his entry into the new state of despair:

> In order to will in despair to be oneself there must be consciousness of the infinite self. This infinite self, however, is really only the abstractest form, the abstractest possibility of the self, and it is this self the man despairingly wills to be, detaching the self from every relation to the Power which posited it, or detaching it from the conception that there is such a Power in existence. (*SUD*, 108–109)

The recurrent vision of immediacy lures Cass again. He flees south to Sambuco, where he finds the externalization of his vision; deciding to stay there, he returns with his family. His life becomes again a drunken nightmare of anxiety (341) and death-wishes (362). He continues to have the same conscience-stricken dream, only the Kierkegaardian "glass case" now becomes an airplane shower stall in which he is executed (368).

In his half-mad state, Cass meets three people who will change his life: Mason Flagg, Luigi Migliori, and Francesca Ricci. Francesca comes to symbolize the vision of happiness for him; he later tells Leverett, "No, I found some kind of *joy* in her, you see—not just pleasure—this joy I felt I'd been searching for all my life, and it was almost enough to preserve my sanity all by itself. *Joy*, you see—a kind of serenity and repose that I never really knew existed" (439–440). And through her, Cass meets the sick Michele, her father, who becomes Cass's chance to escape the torments of his despairing self.

The dream in which Cass had always been guilty of some enormous, nameless crime and had been executed for it had always contained Negroes. Once Cass tells Leverett of this dream: "Ever since I'd been in Europe about half of whatever nightmares I'd had—the ones I remembered, anyway—had been tied up with Negroes. Negroes in prison, Negroes being gassed, me being gassed, Negroes watching me *while* I was being gassed. Like that terrible dream in Paris" (369). Finally in Sambuco, Cass had thought of the repressed origin of his guilt; as a boy he had participated in an act of cruelty to a Negro sharecropper, so for years he had been plagued by a guilty self-hatred. At his meeting with Flagg, Cass had betrayed his guilt by saying, "The only true experience, by God . . . is the one where a man learns to love himself. And his country!" As he later says,

> And as I said these words, and turned around, why so help me God that nightmare I'd had came crashing back like a wave, and then those Negroes and that ruined cabin so long ago and all of that, which seemed to be the symbol of the no-count bastard I'd been all my life, and I became absolutely twisted and wrenched with a feeling I'd never felt before—guilt and homesickness and remorse and pity and combined—all I felt the tears streaming idiotically down my cheeks. (398)

As he struggles to live in his nightmare, Cass is torn between two people. He sees in Francesca the vision of immediacy, and he receives from Flagg the liquor he uses to keep his self drowned. His going to Michele's hut is the incident that tears him from Flagg, for the smell prompts him to think, "It is niggers. The same thing, by God. It is the smell of a black sharecropper's cabin in Sussex County, Virginia. It is the bleeding stink of wretchedness" (416).

Cass immediately grasps at the opportunity to expiate his old guilty by helping the consumptive Michele. Since he has no money, his only method of securing drugs is to ask Flagg for them. Flagg agrees—but only if Cass will virtually become his slave. Cass does anything Flagg asks, for as Cass later says, ". . . the paradox is that this slavish contact with Mason that I had to preserve in order to save Michele freed me to come into that knowledge of selflessness I had thirsted for . . ." (443).

When Francesca is raped and killed, Cass kills Mason, the assumed rapist-murderer. Then he runs from the town, "running not from punishment but as if from the last shred and vestige of the self with which he had been born, . ." (478). Thereafter he hides, until he decides to return home, there to kill his family and himself. On his way to town, he learns of Michele's death, and at that he faints.

As he later remembers, he awakened in the police station with but one idea, "And that was that I should be punished . . ." (490) He wills in his despair to be himself, but Luigi shows Cass the solution. To Cass's pleas for judgment, Luigi shouts, "You *sin* in your guilt!" (494), thereby applying the Kierkegaardian definition of sin; "Sin is this: before God, or with the conception of God, to be in despair at not willing to be oneself, or in despair at willing to be oneself" (*SUD*, 123). Then Luigi says, "Consider the *good* in yourself!" (499)

When Luigi sets him free, Cass realizes that "the anxiety and the anguish—most of it, anyway—had passed" (499). Whether he is free of despair, he never says; evasively he says only "that as for being and nothingness, the one thing I did know was that

to choose between them was simply to choose being, . . ." (500)
Whatever the state of his soul, Cass Kinsolving is most appropriately named: throughout the novel he struggles desperately to
solve the relationship between his God and himself.

[1] William Styron, *Set This House on Fire* (New York: Random House, 1960). Page references will be incorporated into the text.

[2] Robert Gorham Davis, "Styron and the Students," *Critique*, 3 (Summer 1960): 44.

[3] David L. Stevenson, "Styron and the Fiction of the Fifties," *Critique*, 3 (Summer 1960): 47.

[4] John Howard Lawson, "Styron: Darkness and Fire in the Modern Novel," *Mainstream*, 13 (October 1960): 17.

[5] Ihab Hassan, "The Character of Post-War Fiction in America," *English Journal*, 51 (January 1962): 7.

[6] Sören Kierkegaard, *The Sickness Unto Death*, trans. Walter Lowrie (Princeton: Princeton University Press. 1941). Hereafter, references are included in the text as *SUD*.

Moviegoing
in *The Moviegoer*

ohn Bickerson "Binx" Bolling, narrator of *The Moviegoer* (1961),[1] Walker Percy's first published novel, certainly lives up to the epithet which serves as title. During the eight days of the novel proper, he refers to twelve specific and several unidentified movies and to thirty-seven actors and eight actresses. During the same time, he goes to the movies no less than four times, including a drive-in on Saturday night. His appetite seems indiscriminate: he sees *Panic in the Streets*, with Richard Widmark, on Wednesday night, an unidentified western on Thursday night, *Fort Dobbs*, with Clint Walker, on Saturday night, and *The Young Philadelphians*, with Paul Newman, on the following Monday night. The reader soon accepts as true the confession that Binx makes early in his narration: "The fact is I am quite happy in a movie, even a bad movie" (7).

It is not surprising that several commentators have spoken of the role of the movies in the novel.[2] Despite considerable critical interest, though, there has been no extended study of moviegoing as the central theme. Such a study must begin with the realization that Binx has not always been an avid moviegoer:

Until recent years, I read only 'fundamental' books, that is, key books on key subjects, such as *War and Peace*, the novel of novels; *A Study of History*, the solution of the problem of time; Schroedinger's *What is Life?*, Einstein's *The Universe as I See It*, and such. During those years I stood outside the universe and sought to understand it. I lived in my room as an Anyone living Anywhere and read fundamental books and only for diversion took walks around the neighborhood and saw an occasional movie. Certainly it did not matter to me where I was when I read such a book as *The Expanding Universe*. The greatest success of this enterprise, which I call my vertical search, came one night when I sat in a hotel room in Birmingham and read a book called *The Chemistry of Life*. When I finished it, it seemed to me that the main goals of my search were reached or were in principle reachable, whereupon I went out and saw a movie called *It Happened One Night* which was itself very good: A memorable night. The only difficulty was that though the universe had been disposed of, I myself was left over. There I lay in my hotel room with my search over yet still obliged to draw one breath and then the next. But now I have undertaken a different kind of search, a horizontal search. As a consequence, what takes place in my room is less important. What is important is what I shall find when I leave my room and wander in the neighborhood. Before, I wandered as a diversion. Now I wander seriously and sit and read as a diversion.(69–70)[3]

The vertical search fails Binx because of the methodology employed by such "fundamental" books as *The Expanding Universe* and *The Chemistry of Life*. Binx's experience of suffering alienation from his immediate world by virtue of his practice of the scientific method is very reminiscent of twentieth-century existential/phenomenological charges against the practitioners of objectivism. The methodology of scientific empiricism, using ever more elaborate, complicated technology for the gathering of data, enables its practitioners to make ever broader and more penetrating generalizations about the nature of things. But scientific methodology, often thought these days to be the primary, indeed the only, apprehension of reality, actually considers a thing "stripped of all instrumentality," as Jean-Paul Sartre, one of Percy's formative influences, puts it, in *Being and Nothingness*.[4] By "instrumentality" Sartre means that a human being considers a thing originally as it relates to him as a tool, an instrument, a utensil, and then only secondarily as it is a composition of properties and characteristics. Thus science tempts its practitioners to reverse modes of apprehension, indeed finally to forget the specific existence of the thing, all the more to concentrate upon its objective qualities. Then a thing would have, in Sartre's words, "purely external relations,"[5] so that it would appear in exteriority as distant and separate as a star in the sky.

But, in the consideration of a thing, if instrumentality is left out, then man is left over, for it is, after all, man to whom the thing as instrument has referred. No doubt this exclusion of man from a binding relationship with the things which he sees accounts for the widespread feeling that Western man seems more and more alienated from his world even as he develops the technology to quantify it with greater and greater precision. Binx, as a reader of "fundamental" books, learns to measure the immensities of space, but discovers himself to be "left over," as he says, or "*de trop*,"[6] "superfluous," as Sartre puts it.

Even though denied by the scientific-empirical technique and its hoard of data, Binx accepts his "exile" (89). All that he can establish is that he is *not* the object that fascinates him, the world, so he lives in Sartre's state of "fascination": "In fascination there is nothing more than a gigantic object in a desert world. Yet the fascinated intuition is in no way a *fusion* with the object. In fact the condition necessary for the existence of fascination is that the object be raised in absolute relief on a background of emptiness; that is, I am precisely the immediate negation of the object and nothing but that."[7] Binx's search thus becomes "horizontal," as he begins to wander a "*desert world*" or "a world without men,"[8] a world of space, rather than place.

Obsessed by his fascination, which he calls "wonder," Binx moves to the middle class suburb of Gentilly, "a desert if there ever was one," says Percy in an interview.[9] Out there, "where the world is all sky" (73), Binx has "lived ever since, solitary and in wonder, wondering day and night, never a moment without wonder" (42). What he likes about Gentilly, where he lives in an apartment "as impersonal as a motel room" (78), is that his street, Elysian Fields, "is very spacious and airy and seems truly to stretch out like a field under the sky" (10).

Out there he organizes his life around emptiness. He seeks the "deserted playground" (10) of a church across the street from his apartment for his evening ritual of studying the newspaper movie page for his night's outing. It does not matter to him, if the theater is nearly empty, though he does cultivate the acquaintance of theater employees, for their familiarity offers a boundary to his emptiness: "If I did not talk to the theater owner or the ticket seller, I should be lost, cut loose metaphysically speaking. I should be seeing one copy of a film which might be shown anywhere and at any time. There is a danger of slipping clean out of space and time" (75). With that anchor of the known, he can range in the deserts of his fancy, as he does when he talks with the movie cashier about her son: "He is stationed in Arizona and he hates the desert. I am sorry to hear this because I would like it out there very much" (74). Similarly, he can sit in his office, the sphere of the known, and read his one-book library (78), *Arabia Deserta;* hiding the book inside a Standard and Poor binder, Binx offers a telling action, for he is the outwardly successful businessman who really conceives of himself as a ghost wandering a deserted space.[10] He stresses this identification when he reveals his response to *Fort Dobbs,* the movie that he sees at the drive-in, under the stars: "in the movie we are in the desert. There under the black sky rides Clint Walker alone. He is a solitary sort and a wanderer" (143).

Percy does not make a random choice when he selects *It Happened One Night* as the movie for Binx to see just after he has disposed of the world by generalization, but finds himself left over in fact. The very title itself is significant: "it," the "it" of the "I"—"It" dichotomy, the overwhelming *en-soi,* did happen that night, when Binx concluded that the material world was all and that he was nothing. Beyond the suggestiveness of the title, however, is a reference to that particular movie in an essay which Percy had written just about the time that he was writing *The Moviegoer.* In "The Man on the Train: Three Existential Modes,"[11] Percy discusses the problem that contemporary alienated man has with time. Simply stated, Percy's thesis is as follows: contemporary man all too often feels that his life is inauthentic, is immersed in "everydayness." In "everydayness," a term borrowed from Martin Heidegger's majestic *Being and Time,* man falls into a "they-self" system, in which he accepts the standards of the public—the public media, the public institutions, the public worldview—in place of any reflective conception of himself. He listens to what "they say"; he does what "they do." He deliberately hides within the swarming mass of society by doing nothing to distinguish himself from the average, the typical, the ordinary, the acceptable. If he has a vague apprehension that his life is actually without meaning and substance, then he casts about for an alternative.

The only real alternative would of course be to confront the unsatisfactoriness of the present, to struggle for authenticity by an acknowledgement of one's alienation, but it seems to be much more common that the sufferer looks to either the future or the past for the meaning that will transform the present. If he turns to the future, he values the rotation, the orientation toward the radically different future that enables the sufferer to ignore the dreary present. If he turns to the past, he attempts to discover the point at which his life got off the track, in the hope that he could go back to resume his life at that point. This pondering of the past is called repetition. Both of these terms, *rotation* and *repetition,* are familiar in existential literature.

In "The Man on the Train" Percy uses *It Happened One Night* to illustrate rotation, which is alternately called "zone crossing." There is, to begin with, the subject/object split. If we accept the assertion that the subject is nothing but that which observes, then we are left with the subject entirely dependent upon the object, which only overwhelms and bores. What, though, if the subject could vary the object that he observes? Then he would have novelty, would not be bored, could perhaps convince himself that in some new surrounding he would discover the possibility of being something himself. It is vitally important for the alienated man, then, to be able to cross zones, escape from one environment in order to pursue possibility in another, "pass on impassible as a ghost" (*MB*, 88).

Zone crossing, then, is the kind of wandering that Binx decides to do, once he has discovered that the scientific method has excluded him from his world. He will of course view any new object as a part of the "gigantic object in a desert world"; incapable of any "fusion with the object," he will apprehend his world as he views a movie. In *Being and Having,* Gabriel Marcel, another of Percy's influences, establishes a very similar metaphor.[12] There are two modes of detachment: the one of the saint, the other of the spectator. The saint participates in the very core of reality by his indifference to the manifest appearance of the universe. The spectator is characterized by a curiosity, "a form of lust" about the "'cinematographic' representation" imposed on the universe by the scientific technique, and thus "alienation" occurs. "I am not watching a show," Marcel promises to remind himself daily, but Binx Bolling deliberately chooses that behavior. In the novel, then, moviegoing characterizes the alienated man's fascinated gaze at a distant reality, stresses the sense of apartness that he feels.[13]

Binx himself quite obviously understands moviegoing as a symbolic action that illustrates his relationship to the objective-empirical world. On occasion, as when he sees *Panic in the Streets*, he seeks the apparently reassuring—but ultimately deadly—confirmation of his own experience that a scientific formulation offers; this objective "proof" of subjective apprehension Binx calls "certification": "Nowadays when a person lives somewhere, in a neighborhood, the place is not certified for him. More than likely he will live there sadly and the emptiness which is inside him will expand until it evacuates the entire neighborhood. But if he sees a movie which shows his very neighborhood, it becomes possible for him to live, for a time at least, as a person who is Somewhere and not Anywhere" (63).

Generally, though, Binx seeks movies that present patterns of rotational behavior that he might emulate, as for example *Fort Dobbs* or an unnamed movie that he has recently seen: "The movie was about a man who lost his memory in an accident and as a result lost everything: his family, his friends, his money. He found himself a stranger in a strange city. Here he had to make a fresh start, find a new place to live, a new job, a new girl" (4). Such movies stimulate the fantasies that Binx concocts for himself and a girl observed on a bus: "If it were a movie, I would have only to wait. The bus would get lost or the city would be bombed and she and I would tend the wounded" (13).

The devising of zone crossings is now Binx's basic effort in life; by night he goes to the movies and by day he lusts after his secretary, Sharon, sexual novelty being the highest rotation. If all else than himself is the "It," to which he cannot really be joined, then seduction, laying hands upon a part of that "It," would be a delightful pretense that he can in fact touch his world. When they go off for the weekend to the Gulf Coast, he so fascinates her that she wants only to be touched: "Sharon cleaves to me as if, in staying close, she might not see me" (136), Binx tells us, as he leads Sharon to his mother's supposedly deserted fishing camp. But the family is (surprise!) there, and, rather than the seduction, taking his half-siblings to the movies occupies Binx that night. He shows no disappointment, though, for he has already achieved his intention, in making Sharon acknowledge her availability to be touched. In fact, since rotation concerns anticipation rather than participation, possibility rather than actuality, then her potential seduction is preferable to the *fait accompli:* Binx is ever on the threshold, but does not have to suffer the inevitable disappointment that accompanies the failure to maintain transcendence through the sexual act. Rather, Binx thinks that his being able to please his siblings, especially his afflicted brother Lonnie, and his seeing such an appropriate movie as *Fort Dobbs* are bonuses to an already enormously successful escape from his "everydayness." He sums up his exultation: "A good night: Lonnie happy. . . , this ghost of a theater, a warm Southern night, the Western Desert, and this fine big sweet piece, Sharon." Then he draws his conclusion: "A good rotation. A rotation I define as the experiencing of the new beyond the expectation of the experiencing of the new" (143–44).

Fort Dobbs must be a most rewarding experience for Binx, for it mirrors his image of himself, presents his life to him as a stylized performance, objectifies his subjectivity (which the subjectivity cannot do for itself, of course). Binx wants to live his life, in other words, as if it were a role in a Western movie. In "The Man on the Train" Percy draws an existential meaning from that classic American genre: "The I-It dichotomy is translated intact in the Western movie. Who is he, this Gary Cooper person who manages so well to betray nothing of himself whatsoever, who is he but I myself, the locus of pure possibility?" (*MB*, 94)

As a moviegoer, Binx is aware that he must employ the appropriate gestures, if he is to impersonate a person of unrealized possibilities, act like the stranger in a Western movie. He assumes the role expected of him on any occasion. Mostly he patterns his behavior after movie stars, those creatures of "resplendent reality" (17), as he characterizes them: "Toward her I keep a Gregory Peckish sort of distance" (68); "it comes back to me how the old Gable used to work at such jobs: he knew how to seem to work and how to seem to forget about women and still move in such a way as to please women: stand asweat with his hand in his back pockets" (95); "It is possible to stand at the window, loosen my collar and rub the back of my neck like Dana Andrews" (105). On an occasion when "everydayness" is vanquished by the novelty of an automobile accident, Binx is able to act like a romantic hero, and he exults: "O Tony. O Rory. You never had it so good with direction. Not even you Bill Holden, my noble Will" (127). For once, Binx feels free of the "malaise," which he defines as "the pain of loss. The world is lost to you, the world and the people in it, and there remains only you and the world and you no more able to be in the world than Banquo's ghost" (120).

Binx's nighttime disguises seem obvious enough, especially since he frequently tells us whom he is impersonating. But he adopts a daytime disguise that he does not acknowledge; this identity purports to be genuine: "I am a model tenant and a model citizen and take pleasure in doing all that is expected of me. My wallet is full of identity cards, library cards, credit cards. . . . It is a pleasure to carry out the duties of a citizen and to receive in return a receipt or a neat styrene card with one's name on it certifying, so to speak, one's right to exist. What satisfaction I take in appearing the first day to get my auto tag and brake sticker! I subscribe to *Consumer Reports* and as a consequence I own a first-class television set, an all but silent air conditioner and a very long lasting deodorant. My armpits never stink. I pay attention to all spot announcements on the radio about mental health, the seven signs of cancer, and safe driving . . ." (6–7).

Such slavish adherence to the model behavior of the consumer. Binx would have us believe that the advertising industry and the communications media invented him! He is making himself into a mechanical man: just as much as Sartre's waiter, he is playing at being what he says he is. Describing a waiter who is elegantly excessive in acting like a waiter, Sartre explains such posturing as the waiter's expression, to the sufficiently perceptive, of his contempt for his own role. There is more to him than just being a waiter; that *more* is his consciousness. He is conscious of himself as a waiter, hence is superior to his actuality, transcends his factual nature.[14] Binx is, in other words, engaged in a pattern of bad faith.[15]

Binx wants to live, then, as a consumer of new products and sensory experiences, but never to chance an authentic emotion. The most that he can tolerate is an occasional bout of the malaise, a weak nausea that signals a revulsion against a confining, threatening world.[16] Yet it is precisely through emotions, even nausea, that Binx could gain reentry to the world denied him by the objectifying media. For it must be an emotion that makes an "I" aware of his facticity, that is, the fact that he exists as an actuality.

Take the emotion of fear, which Heidegger uses as an example in *Being and Time*.[17] Binx acknowledges that in Korea, in combat, while lying wounded, he felt in touch with things and made a vow to search for a meaning for his life, if he lived (10). *Being and Time* would explain his behavior thus: Fear is one of the avenues through which Dasein, the "I," comes to itself or finds itself.[18] Dasein becomes open to the disclosure that it dwells in an existence that is both limiting and limited, and that what it confronts in that confine is of vital significance to it, so that it must be responsible for itself, despite its lack of control over its origin. Fear, then, is an outstanding example of one of the states-of-mind, that ontological characteristic by which Dasein is made aware of the actuality of its placement in the world.

In Korea, Binx had, by virtue of his fear, become aware of himself as a fact. But at the same time, he had vowed a search; hence he possessed not only the mode of the actual but also the mode of the possible. Indeed, the mere knowledge that Dasein knows that a search is possible is proof that *a priori* it knows that it is bound not only to the actual but also to the possible—hence revelation and resolution are partners in our life.[19] Binx lost his resolution when he came home, though, for he chose the wrong kind of search, became immersed in everydayness, experienced "fallenness," yet another characteristic that is innate in the human experience.[20]

On the morning of the opening of the novel Binx acknowledges that for the first time in years he had dreamed of Korea, "woke with the taste of it in my mouth, the queasy-quince taste of 1951 and the Orient" (11). That taste, as he later acknowledges, is fear. Hence Binx has experienced *Befindlichkeit*, the finding of himself in a concrete placement, the strategy of introduction that Percy has repeatedly stated he employs. "Opened" to experience, shocked by a catastrophe into a stunned wakefulness, Binx really looks at his world: "this morning when I got up, I dressed as usual and began as usual to put my belongings into my pockets: wallet, notebook (for writing down occasional thoughts), pencil, keys, handkerchief, pocket slide rule (for calculating percentage returns on principal). They looked both unfamiliar and at the same time full of clues. I stood in the center of the room and gazed at the little pile, sighting through a hole made by thumb and forefinger. What was unfamiliar about them was that I could see them. They might have belonged to someone else. A man can look at this little pile on his bureau for thirty years and never once see it. It is as invisible as his own hand. Once I saw it, however, the search became possible" (11).

The significance of the various objects of Binx's sight is that all are tools, implements, each of which has a specific function for him. In most cases the function is self-evident, the wallet holds his money and cards of identity, for example, but with two tools there are several possible functions to be considered, so Binx specifies (by parenthesis) their personal use. *His* notebook is for jotting down "occasional thoughts"; *his* slide rule is for the calculation of percentages. Moreover the objects were not first perceived as indifferent things unrelated in space, then discovered to have supernumerary characteristics of specific identity, but rather were perceived as a complex of related functions, related to a unique individual. What Binx has discovered is Heidegger's tool complex, which Sartre adopts as the "relation of instrumentality,"[21] the primordial apprehension of being-in-the-world. Through his perception, Binx has realized a system of tasks that refer only to him, that represent his future; he has found himself centered in a world, even as he stands in the center of the room.

Thus Binx experiences the Sartrean "upsurge" of reflection.[22] The complex of tools has referred to a single tool which uses all the other tools. But his existence has not been established in or by an empty world; rather Binx is also the single subject who sees his objectivity while knowing that he is still a subjectivity. Thus he reflects upon a relationship that transcends the subject/object split; he is in a world by virtue of his body, no longer just in an environment as a "ghost in a machine" viewing from afar the "cinematographic representation" that he is not.

We should not, however, expect too much from Binx's upsurge of reflection. It is true that he has placed himself in his unique history after dwelling in public, that is to say, timeless, time. We should not, though, expect a basic change in his behavior, for the original reflective upsurge is in bad faith.[23] The newly reflective Binx may now be aware of himself, but he determines to remain that self by continuing his impersonation. He thinks that he can succeed in this performance because no one else is involved; the genuine reflective revolution is for-others, must be perceived by the Other. Perhaps the only change we may observe will lie not in Binx's behavior (which we know only through his not entirely trustworthy revelation), but in his narration: he should become more ironic as he expresses the essence of consciousness (reflection), which is negation: "In irony a man annihilates what he posits within one and the same act; he leads us to believe in order not to be believed; he affirms to deny and denies to affirm; he creates a positive object but it has no being other than its nothingness."[24]

Outwardly, then, Binx will continue his wandering and wondering. Inwardly, he begins a rather halfhearted search for a meaning for his life. The recognition of one's concrete placement leads to a sensitivity to the factors that determined that placement, one's "thrownness," *Geworfenheit,* as Heidegger calls it.[25] Binx begins to probe his family history, in an effort to account for his own life. On Wednesday, at his aunt's house, he studies the photographs of his father and other male relatives (24–25) and questions his aunt about them (49). All he can conclude is that the older Bollings were "serene in their identities," while his father's eyes betray a trait that Binx knows all too well: "Beyond a doubt they are ironical" (25).

On Thursday night Binx goes to a movie on the chance that it might enable him to achieve a repetition; noticing that a western is playing at the same theater in which he had seen *The Oxbow Incident* fourteen years before, Binx returns to it, to achieve what he avows is "a successful repetition": "the re-enactment of past experience toward the end of isolating the time segment which has lapsed in order that it, the lapsed time, can be savored of itself and without the usual adulteration of events that clog time like peanuts in brittle" (79–80). Perhaps Binx regards the experience as a success because it evoked nostalgia, which he later identifies as "the characteristic mood of repetition" (169–170), but any meaning inherent in the experience, he has to admit, "eluded" him (80). Binx seems unwilling, really, to confront that life fourteen years ago, to admit that it was as fraught with everydayness as the present. In "The Man on the Train" Percy distinguishes between two forms of repetition.

"The aesthetic repetition captures the savor of repetition without surrendering the self as a locus of experience and possibility," he notes, while the existential repetition is a "passionate quest in which the incident serves as a thread in the labyrinth to be followed at any cost" (*MB*,95–96). All Binx seems to experience here is the savoring of the moment, while withholding any real involvement of himself in determining to change his life. His choice of a western seems proof that he is at heart interested foremost in possibility, not actuality.

On Friday Binx devises what would at first seem to be a sincere repetition. He wishes to explore the history of the duck club, "the only relic" (6) of his father that he still possesses; he would seem to want "to stand before the house of one's childhood," as Percy describes repetition in "The Man on the Train."[26] But it turns out that the whole trip to St Bernard Parish, where the club is located, is merely a part of Binx's impersonating Clark Gable in order to fascinate Sharon. Once he gets there, he contents himself to contemplate the money that he will realize from the real estate (89) and to appreciate the very basic sense of ready-to-hand reality displayed by Mr. Sartalamaccia, the builder of a housing development: "I take pleasure in watching him run a thumb over the sawn edges of the sheathing" (93). The conclusion of the outing emphasizes Binx's outer/inner duplicity: "I go home as the old Gable, asweat and with no thought for her and sick to death with desire" (96). That "sick to death" is a nicely couched allusion to Kierkegaard's despair, the malady that really dominates Binx's private life, fueling his desire.

The weekend is dedicated to Sharon's seduction. When that achievement is frustrated, Binx seems to direct his interest to repetition, for he attempts on Sunday morning to discover from his mother something about that fellow sufferer, his dead father (148–49). But his mother has adopted a way of seeing "life, past and present, in terms of a standard comic exaggeration" (151); one reduces all events to the routine—beyond that, one goes to church and fishing. With his exhaustion of both the rotational and the repetitional capacities of the weekend, Binx, not surprisingly, is overwhelmed by the malaise on the trip back to town (166).

At that point in the novel, Binx becomes, literally, the man on the train. He is obliged to attend a convention in Chicago, so he and Kate, who invites herself along, take the Sieur Iberville on Sunday night. Such a jaunt is suffused with expectancy; like Thomas Wolfe before him, Binx knows "the peculiar gnosis of trains," recognizes the train as an "eminence from which there is revealed both the sorry litter of the past and the future bright and simple as can be" and also as a vehicle that facilitates zone crossing, "one's privileged progress through the world" (184).

The success of rotation depends, though, upon the moviegoer's continued seclusion of himself in "unrisked possibility" or his ability to embody the stylized behavior of the stars whom he impersonates, that is, really act with gestural perfection. On the train Binx is caught in a situation in which he would like to display for Kate the sexual prowess of Clark Gable in his role as Rhett Butler. His failure is dismal, as he confesses to another of his ideals, Rory Calhoun (199).[27]

But Kate, rather than fault him for his impotence, his failure to live up to his impersonation, accepts him in his reduced humanity and takes care of him (201, 202, 206). Having the night before confessed that she regarded him as the "unmoved mover" (197), Kate demonstrates her faith in him as he is, and as a consequence Binx is serene in his own identity for once in his life. Thus he is free of the sexual desire that has haunted him for years as the symbol of possibility: "What an experience, Rory, to be free of it for once. Rassled out. What a sickness it is, Rory, this latter-day post-Christian sex. To be pagan it would be one thing, an easement taken easily in a rosy old pagan world; to be Christian it would be another thing, fornication forbidden and not even to be thought of in the new life, and I can see that it need not be thought of if there were such a life. But to be neither pagan nor Christian but this: oh this is a sickness, Rory" (207).

Because of the love for him exhibited by Kate's taking care of him, Binx feels more of a communion, more at ease than ever before in his life. *The Young Philadelphians* (its very title suggesting agape, not eros), the movie that Binx and Kate go to see in Chicago, mirrors Binx's new found tranquillity and optimism:

> Kate holds my hand tightly in the dark.
> Paul Newman is an idealistic young fellow who is disillusioned and becomes cynical and calculating. But in the end he recovers his ideals. (211)

Such happy endings occur only in the movies, though. Both Kate and Binx emerge from the theater with a foreboding, which is fulfilled by a call from Aunt Emily, who condemns Binx's feckless behavior with Kate. Once again Binx becomes the man on the train (except that, no trains being scheduled, he is actually the man on the bus). Despite the prospect of the interview with his aunt, Binx is in reasonably good spirits. He reads *Arabia Deserta* and enjoys the sights—and watches over the sleeping Kate. His mixed activities suggest the two directions his life may take: a return to his ghostly wandering or an acceptance of the care-relation.

Part of the trip is occupied by Binx's observation of two fellow passengers, each of whom personifies an extreme of human behavior. There is, first, a romantic, a young college graduate so captivated by the ideal that he will find it extremely difficult ever to settle for the actual. Binx concludes that the romantic is "a moviegoer, though of course he does not go to the movies" (216), that is, that the boy has excluded himself from the world by his very way of looking at it. There is, second, a salesman, who lives in a world of total actuality, who creates his world by the things he can touch: "he gives me a sample of his product, a sample ell of tempered and blued steel honed to a two-edged blade. Balancing it in his hand, he tests its heft and temper. The hand knows the blade, practices its own metaphysic of the goodness of the steel" (216). He does not suffer any alienation at all, Binx knows, but neither does he possess any sense of the difference between himself and his environment: "Businessmen are our only metaphysicians, but the trouble is, they are one-track metaphysicians" (217).[28]

When Binx stands before his aunt, he has achieved a degree of confidence that he has never before felt. But her contempt for his behavior brutally erodes the faith in himself that Kate's love had given him; Aunt Emily's last question, particularly, demonstrates her judgment: "What do you think is the purpose of life—to go to the movies and dally with every girl that comes along?" (226) Binx rejects that interpretation of his character, but he can offer nothing to contradict it. Thus he stumbles off, to relapse into the very behavior his aunt had described. Thinking that Kate has seen the wisdom of her stepmother's view and therefore cast him adrift, Binx is desperate to find a woman, merge his nothingness in the only kind of being that he can enter.[29] He calls Sharon, appealing to his guardian angel for help: "I've got to find her, Rory" (239). Failing to contact her, he frantically settles for her roommate Joyce, whom he tries to fascinate by impersonating Marlon Brando (230). At that moment, on the verge of falling back into his most alienated form, he spies Kate who has not betrayed him after all. They renew their intention to marry, and Binx dares to hope: "Is it possible that it is not too late?" (231).

The Epilogue offers evidence of a year's success. Binx has entered medical school; thus he undertakes a genuine repetition, for he dares to resume the way of life which fatally alienated his father and which had excluded him from his own world for all of his adult life. He has remained faithful in caring for Kate, who seems to feel that she exists only because he constantly thinks of her. He mentions no movies that he has seen, nor does he affect the behavior of any movie star. Binx Bolling has come out of the movies, to chance acting himself.

[1](New York: Noonday Press, 1967). Page references will be incorporated into the text.
[2]In her essay "The Moviegoer of the 1950's [*Twentieth Century Literature*, 19 (July 1968): 84–89] Mary Thale emphasizes the irony that Binx cultivates to separate himself from his fellow citizens of the Eisenhower era, who have been reduced to stereotypical behavior by such media as the movies. In "Walker Percy's Indirect Communications"

[*Texas Studies in Language and Literature*, 11 (Spring 1969): 867–900] I argue that Binx realizes that the movies seem to provide the kind of transcendent experience for the contemporary world that the religious institution once provided. Scott Byrd, in "Mysteries and Movies" [*Mississippi Quarterly*, 25 (Spring 1972): 165–181], discusses the references to the various movie stars in the novel, pointing out that Binx likens a person to a movie star in order to deny that person's reality and likens himself to a movie star whenever he is acting deceptively. Harvey R. Greenberg, M.D. [*The Movies on Your Mind* (New York: Saturday Review Press, 1975), 4] also discusses Binx's personality, approaching it from the direction of psychology: "One encounters chronic moviemania in rigid, inhibited types who feel exquisitely uncomfortable when forced into close interpersonal contact. Safe only in well-defined social situations, intolerably anxious if called upon to improvise, these people sleepwalk through the day's routine and only come alive at second hand, as proxy participants in the adventures of their screen idols. (Walker Percy's elegant novel *The Moviegoer* describes such a case.)" More recently, Simone Vauthier, in "Title as Microtext" [*Journal of Narrative Technique*, 5 (September 1975): 219–29], has asserted that the title announces "a complex metaphor for man's ambivalent relation to experience," a generalization with great potential, but not quite sufficiently supported by analysis. The only treatment unsympathetic to the use of the moviegoing materials is that of Alfred Kazin ["The Pilgrimage of Walker Percy," *Harper's Magazine*, 243 (June 1971): 81–86], who thinks that the title is misleading because the novel is "not exactly about going to the movies." Still, though, Kazin feels that the movie material, if it must be used, is a device that reveals Binx's basically positive nature: "He has become the one man around him who seems to want nothing for himself but to look, to be a spectator in the dark. This clinician and diagnostician of the soul trains himself in the movies. The enlarged, brilliantly lighted and concentrated figures upon the screen have taught him how to focus on the secret human places." The present essay differs with Kazin's interpretation.

³To help us understand these generalizations, Binx describes on another occasion a fellow student who had mastered the vertical search: "He was absolutely unaffected by the singularities of time and place. His abode was anywhere. It was all the same to him whether he catheterized a pig at four o'clock in the afternoon in New Orleans or at midnight in Transylvania. He was actually like one of those scientists in the movies who don't care about anything but the problem in their heads—now here is a fellow who . . . will be heard from. Yet I do not envy him. I would not change places with him if he discovered the cause and cure of cancer. For he is no more aware of the mystery which surrounds him than a fish is aware of the water it swims in. He could do research for a thousand years and never have an inkling of it" (51–52). Binx is here employing the distinction between *problem* and *mystery* made by Gabriel Marcel, in *Being and Having*, trans. Katherine Farrer, (New York: Harper and Row, 1965), 100–01: "Distinguish between the Mysterious and the Problematic. A problem is something met with which bars my passage. It is before me in its entirety. A mystery, on the other hand, is something in which I find myself caught up, and whose essence is therefore not before me in its entirety. It is as though in this province the distinction between *in me* and *before me* loses its meaning.

"The Natural. The province of the Natural is the same as the province of the Problematic. We are tempted to turn mystery into problem.

"The Mysterious and Ontological are identical. There is a mystery of knowledge which belongs to the ontological order (as Maritain saw) but the epistemologist does not know this, makes a point of ignoring it, and turns it into a problem."

⁴Jean-Paul Sartre, *Being and Nothingness*, trans. Hazel E. Barnes, (New York:

Philosophical Library, 1956), 200. Percy defines his relationship to Sartre in the interview with Charles T. Bunting, "An Afternoon with Walker Percy," *Notes on Mississippi Writers*, 4 (Fall 1971):43–61.

[5] Sartre, 200.

[6] *Ibid.*, 84.

[7] *Ibid.*, 176–177.

[8] *Ibid.*, 307.

[9] John Carr, "Rotation and Repetition: Walker Percy," in *Kite-Flying and Other Irrational Acts* (Baton Rouge: Louisiana State University Press, 1972), 48.

[10] Percy seems obviously to be alluding to Gilbert Ryle's grumpy description of the modern concern with the isolated subjectivity as "the dogma of the Ghost in the Machine." See Ryle's *The Concept of Mind* (London: Hutchinson's University Library, 1949), 15–16ff, for an illustration of the "commonsense" reaction to phenomenological or existential stress on the significance of the subjective. See also my "Time and Eternity in *The Moviegoer*," *Southern Humanities Review*, 16 (Spring 1982): 129–141, for the distinction between space and place, time and eternity, in the novel.

[11] *Partisan Review*, 23 (Fall 1956): 478–494. Reprinted in *The Message in the Bottle* (New York: Farrar, Straus, and Giroux, 1975): 83–100, Percy's selected essays on language.

[12] Marcel, *Being and Having*, 18–21.

[13] See my "Walker Percy's *The Moviegoer*: the Cinema as Cave," *Southern Studies*, 19 (Winter 1980); 331–354, for a discussion of Platonism as a source of alienation.

[14] Sartre, 59–60.

[15] *Ibid.*, 48–54.

[16] *Ibid.*, 338–39.

[17] Martin Heidegger, *Being and Time*, trans. John Macquarrie and Edward Robinson (New York: Harper and Row, 1962), 179–82.

[18] *Ibid.*, 391–96.

[19] *Ibid.*, 182–95.

[20] *Ibid.*, 219–24.

[21] Heidegger, 134–48.

[22] Sartre, 153.

[23] *Ibid.*, 161.

[24] *Ibid.*, 47.

[25] Heidegger, 174.

[26] *The Message in the Bottle*, 96. A significant point is reached in *The Last Gentleman*, when Will Barrett, having returned to the South after a sojourn in the land of the objective-empiricists, literally does stand before the house of his father.

[27] Binx's choice of Rory Calhoun, a relatively little-known movie actor, as his personification of sexual gestural perfection is explained by the revelation in *Parade* (23 October 1977): 1: "When actress Lita Baron bitterly divorced Rory Calhoun six years ago, she alleged that her husband had committed adultery with Betty Grable and 78 other women." Binx has apparently been a student not merely of moviegoing but also of movie goings-on.

[28] The tension between a purely abstract and a purely concrete view of the world remains the major structure of Percy's fictional world. Will Barrett is drawn between life as an engineer and life as a car dealer. Tom More suffers his fall because he foolishly attempts to resolve the tension between angelism and bestialism by technology. Lance Lamar, having lost the romantic-abstract view when Lucy died, opts for the concrete-genital view with Margot.

[29]The notebook of Suter Vaught, in *The Last Gentleman*, explains much of the sexual activity that occurs or at least is thought about in Percy's novels. Sexual activity for Percy's characters is not a determined behavior (manifesting a generic energy), but a chosen behavior (manifesting an individual's desire to expand into his *en-soi*); it is more (or at least as much) a phenomenological than a physiological search. See also *Lost in the Cosmos* (New York: Farrar, Straus, and Giroux, 1983), for Percy's argument that much of modern man's frantic sexual behavior results from his ontological distress.

Old Fish Hawk:
From Stereotype to Archetype

*M*itchell F. Jayne's *Old Fish Hawk* (1970)[1] continues the traditional theme in white American literature that the men of the dark castes have a valuable wisdom to offer the sons of the white caste. These red and black men have been pictured as having necessarily retained a greater reverence for the natural and human world than have the victorious whites, whose material success has prompted them to measure all experience in terms of power and property. Such disparate classic texts as *Uncle Remus, His Songs and His Sayings* (1880) and *The Adventures of Huckleberry Finn* (1885) have as a basic strategy the education of a young white by an older black. Joel Chandler Harris creates the kindly Uncle Remus, who uses the beast fables of black folklore to teach his little white visitor that all human beings have the same basic range of emotions. So, too, does Mark Twain use Nigger Jim, to demonstrate to Huckleberry that even a slave loves, suffers shame, and has the capacity for bravery and self-sacrifice. More recently William Faulkner, in *Go Down, Moses* (1942), has described the rituals through which Sam Fathers, an old man of mixed red and black origin, teaches Isaac McCaslin, an heir to the Southern plantation system, the universal human values.

In Jayne's novel the Fish Hawk, an Osage who suddenly discovers that he has exceeded the Scriptural three score and ten, allows Corby Boggs to accompany him on a hunt. In the woods he induces the boy to a recognition that, while there are times when one may take from nature, there are also times when one should give back or forebear to take in the first place. But the old Indian is not introduced as such a venerable figure, invested with the power to perform such an archetypal, priest-like function. Rather he is viewed by others as the stereotyped Indian, a shiftless drunk, and so he views himself. He has been content to accept that definition, for he has pretty nearly forgotten his racial heritage and he has felt that life is endless and therefore meaningless. It will take a succession of deaths—his dog Ebo's, the bear's, his friend Charlie's, and the boar's—to complete his realization that his life will soon end and that his having lived at all will be significant only if he passes on his experience, his store of Indian experience. In so doing he comes to realize the significance of the action of his father, who spent the last few days before his execution simply talking to his son. The Fish Hawk thus begins to see that life is a continuity, that there is a coming-in and a going-out. He must therefore initiate Corby Boggs, not merely for Corby's sake, but to honor his long dead father and his own sojourn on this earth.

The Fish Hawk has lived the last ten years in Bent's Ford, a southwest Missouri village which survives by providing services for the neighboring farmers. Living stark lives in direct, intense struggle with the ground they work, the farmers have no reverence for the woods or the animals within them—the forest is simply a refuge for beasts that prey upon their crops and their stock. When, toward the end, the Fish Hawk returns without having killed the destructive bear, implying that it would be dead of old age within weeks and that its pilferage ought to be borne for that period, the whites simply cannot conceive of the idea that such a sacrifice of property would be fitting. The area is sparsely settled, so the Fish Hawk has been able to build a succession of squatter camps without being evicted by the whites. The landscape of the area is mostly forested and hilly; he can hunt for food and for the plants with which he can barter. What little money he earns is gained by serving the whites as the doctor and trainer of their animals; it is only because of his competence in these roles that "the community of Bent's Ford put up with his periodic carousals" (19).

In the opening of the novel the Fish Hawk is in the midst of one of those carousals. Having drunk nearly a quart of whiskey, he staggers up the street of the town toward the only hotel, where the proprietor and two drummers sit on the veranda. It is a late summer night, and both the season and the hour comment upon the old man: as the late summer tempts anyone to consider it an endless dream, so the Fish Hawk is unheeding about his life as having an end, and so, too, is his drunken vision as dim and indistinct as the shadowy night.

If it is late for the Fish Hawk, so, too, it is late for all Indians: the time of the novel suggests that the Fish Hawk is to be viewed not merely as an individual, but as a representative of the red race. According to Deut Boggs (143), Uncle Ben Thrail-kill had seen the imported Russian boars in 1858, thirty-five years before; thus the time is the summer of 1893. Up in Chicago, on July 12 of that year, the young historian Frederick Jackson Turner was optimistically announcing that though the frontier was in fact closed, it had bequeathed certain gracious qualities, chief among them love of freedom, to white American character. Nearby, at the Columbian Exposition, the "youngest Indian slayer of the Plains,"[2] Colonel William F. Cody, was demonstrating, in his most triumphant tour, that the frontier remained open in the way that white Americans really conceived it, as a world of simplistic violence. White Americans were, in other words, attempting to generalize about what the red man had really meant to the white man. But any interpretation, from "noble savage" to "just plain savage," ignored the surviving Indian, who was in danger of living as a useless relic, forgetting his past, and dying out from despair and drunkenness.

Even drunk, the Fish Hawk projects an awesome image to the city men: "From where the men sat on the porch, the figure looked like an apparition. A tall man, wrapped in a reddish blanket, with a flap-brimmed hat holding the face in shadow. The two salesmen, when they were this far out in the back woods, suffered the city man's insecurity in seeing the edge of wild land . . . the jumping off place into yesterday. The short fat man who had spoken felt a strange prickle of fear at the silence with which the stranger had appeared" (2).

By speaking with a slurred voice and by shuffling his feet, as he waits for acceptance, the Fish Hawk himself destroys the awe that the drummers had felt toward him. He announces himself, in other words, as a stereotype; he is the drunk Indian—if not a good Indian, according to the white frontier saying, at least a tolerable Indian. As Joke Bryan, the innkeeper, explains to the salesmen: "Aw hell, . . . he's just an old Indian relic, got left over from early times. Don't know how he keeps alive, much as he drinks. He helps with stock and doctors hound dogs and such-like. He don't do any harm" (3).

But the Fish Hawk is bolder than usual, because of his drunkenness. When one drummer whispers, "That old man looks like he'd have your scalp off for a nickel," the Fish Hawk, overhearing him, replies, "You're behin' the times. . . . Been any way fifty years since an Indian took a scalp in these parts, . . . maybe sixty, I never kep' much track. But I don't know of any of 'em would have cut yours, no more hair than you've got" (4). When he offers the two of them a drink from his bottle, they pay only lip service to it, and he observes, "Huh! . . . It's sure hard to see how you all ended up with the country, and the Injuns ended up with nothin'." Then, as an implied excuse for his condition, he explains that he had received the whiskey as payment for a job: "Always whisky. Nobody pays cash money nowadays for nothing, leasewise not to me."

This complaint leaves an opening for the white man, who has been smarting from the rebuke offered his race by "this tall caricature of an Indian": "Tell you what, old man, . . . I got fifty cents here says you can't show us what a war dance is like. Me and Bill here, we can beat on the banister and make like drums. How about it?" For a moment the Fish Hawk remembers a white man who had tried to rob him of his horses fifty years before and whom he had killed, but he was unhorsed long ago and now he is willing to allow the salesman to rob him of his last shred of dignity: "The Indian stepped back and slowly began to shuffle his feet in rhythm to the beat. It was ludicrous; at the end of four beats he would lift his gaunt shanks like an ancient crane, first one leg, then the other" (6). When Joke Bryan's wife comes out to intervene, the Fish Hawk actually conspires in his own humiliation, as if he were on the midway with Colonel Cody: "Evenin', Miz Bryan, . . . just doing a little war dance for the dudes here; cash money. See the old Osage warrior cut a caper, come one, come all!" Then he passes out. A ritual of superiority in a warrior world is transformed into a ritual of inferiority in a commercial world. The frontier is indeed closed, and the only place for the Indian in a white world would seem to be the side show.

The Fish Hawk wakes up in a cell, where he has been allowed to sleep by Billy Firman, the town marshal. The implication is apt; that the Fish Hawk would have been put in jail for lodging is perfectly plausible, but beyond that, it is a comment upon the state of his life; he is in a prison of the present and of stereotype. Even Billy Firman, who shares old age with the Fish Hawk and is fond of him, fails to see him as an individual: "I always heard about Indians drinkin' and I'll be dipped if I don't believe it's true, bein' around you" (17). Subdued by a headache, the Fish Hawk tries to separate himself from an abstraction: "How many Indians have you known?" Billy refuses to distinguish: "Nary one, 'cept you, . . . and that's plenty, by God." In his characteristic way, the Fish Hawk observes that both he and his race suffer by reflection: "Some dogs kill sheep, . . . and some people are fools, and some Indians drink, I reckon. You just happen to know a dumb Indian who don't know how much to drink" (18).

The two old men linger in the shade of a tree, to be joined by the town half-wit, Towsack Charlie, so called because he gathers empty bottles for a living, whose family had years before abandoned him as it went on west. The Fish Hawk is more than a little fond of the retarded man, who is only a boy in behavior. Although the Fish Hawk later concludes that his closeness to Charlie was based on the fact that they both were "sort of the town misfits or something" (170), the real basis for his affection might be a trait he attributes to the Osages without recognizing that it would therefore apply to himself. Speaking to Mrs. Bryan, he says: "The People, . . . my people—that is, the

Osages—they took care of their own, both the fatherless children and the dead" (169). Even though he has long since ceased to be conscious of most of his heritage, the Fish Hawk still acts out its customs, some of which are, ultimately, not just tribal, but archetypal.

Without realizing it, in short, he fulfills the role of father for Charlie. Puzzling over his real father's flight, Charlie asks the Fish Hawk about the treatment that he had received from his father, particularly, "Did you Pa ever whup ye?" "Not hardly," says the Fish Hawk. "He took me to Clarksville when the soldiers took him, and he used to talk to me every day, tell me what an Osage was expected to do and how he ought to live, but he never whipped me" (24). Almost before he knows it, the Fish Hawk tells the story of his father's execution as a hostage and of his own adoption as an eight-year-old by a sergeant, fittingly named Parsons. He realizes that the white man had fulfilled the role of father without attempting to supplant the Fish Hawk's real father (or racial identity): "They took me to raise, . . . him and his wife, and I went to school with the other children at the fort. I wore a button shirt and shoes, but I never cut my hair. Sergeant Parsons told me I could wear it long to honor my Pa, and I never have cut it shorter than it is right now, on account of that" (26). Continuing to tell Charlie of the past, the Fish Hawk seems almost to understand that he is engaged in a ritual, for he is drawn to ritual behavior; having drunk the coffee given him by Billy Firman, "The old man looked within the blue cup, poured the dregs on the ground as if he fulfilled some ancient rite by doing it" (30).

The spell is broken by the arrival of the drunken Marcus Boggs, who immediately restores the Fish Hawk to his stereotype: "Hello, Fish Hawk, you damn old jug-sucker!" The bottle is passed, and passed. Billy is "disturbed" at the interruption of the Fish Hawk's story, annoyed that "for a while he had seen the Fish Hawk in a different light" (36) and that the Indian's relapse is so immediate. Marcus has come to hire him to kill a bear that is raiding his son Deut's farm; the Fish Hawk is flattered to be viewed as a hunter, tempted all the more when Marcus says that part of the pay will be " a gallon of Injun liniment" (35). The Indian agrees and starts to his camp to get his dog and traps, but he is aware that Charlie still has something bothering him, so he allows the afflicted man to walk along. Charlie reveals that he cannot get death off his mind and that he has devised his own rituals to ease his passage: "If you got religion, . . . you got a reason for everything. You can explain away anything happens, like Miz Bryan does, on account of the Lord intended it; like Mary Lou gettin' the scarlet fever and dyin'." But, Charlie, confesses, "I'm not right bright, . . . so I don't understand that. I just want to be doctored good and buried right" (43).

At his camp, the Fish Hawk carefully assembles the gear that he will need. Like a Hemingway character, he is aware of the magic of ritual preparation: "Unwrapping a small buckskin parcel from his pouch, the Fish Hawk poured ten of the heavy 45-70 cartridges onto the spread canvas in which he stored the rifle. He wiped each of the brass cylinders with an oily cloth, inspected the lead domes of the bullets to pick out the truest-looking ones." Even so, he is aware, his studied behavior does not approach the magic of the past: "It wasn't, he thought, like the old days, when a man measured his powder, cut his patches, knew to the hair how much wadding to use with his own gun. The cartridges were better, of course, drier and more uniform, and the sealed primers were better than the old caps, which might deform under the hammer, or be defective. But each of the brass cylinders was an uncertainty, a thing put together by men unknown in a distant palce, men who couldn't know or care what one true shot might mean. It was one more missing ritual, the art of loading the gun" (46).

On the trip to the Boggs farm, the Fish Hawk happens upon the bear, but before he can get close enough for a good shot, the bear is scared off. The source of its alarm is Corby Boggs, an eleven-year-old. The Fish Hawk is at once taken with the boy's mien: "He looked at the Fish Hawk with frank surprise, but there was no hint of either fear or intimidation in his blue eyes. It was the look of a child who neither supposed nor anticipated evil, and took each event as it happened, with aplomb and a calm wonder" (54). Having lived in isolation with only his family, Corby is awkward with the Fish Hawk, depending upon the stereotype provided by his father: "You're wanting to get to whisky, ain't you?" The Fish Hawk, accustomed to such diminution, yet peevish because the question is accurate, asks why he would say such a thing. Innocence replies: "Pa said . . . you wouldn't scratch your ass without you had a drink."

When Deut Boggs obviously defers to the woods knowledge of the Indian, Corby's first impression of the Fish Hawk proves inadequate. The Indian has impressed the boy, who attempts to get a more accurate understanding of him, even though he accepts low status by lodging and taking meals in the barn. Discarding the "drunk Indian" stereotype, Corby wants to romanticize the Fish Hawk as a "savage Indian": "You ever killed anybody?" Although he had killed a thief fifty years before, the Fish Hawk apparently understands that a young boy might not be able to distinguish between those times of necessity and these of fantasy, for he replies that he has not. Helpfully, Corby gives him another chance: "not even one man? . . . Like a soldier or a settler?" The Fish Hawk hedges this time: "As fur as I know, . . . I've never killed anybody. My folks were hunters, not fighters, . ." (66). Thus Corby learns more about the Fish Hawk and the Osages; just as importantly, there is a refusal to glorify death by violence that anticipates the Fish Hawk's later action.

While Corby may have begun to see the Fish Hawk in a different way, the Indian continues to see himself as the drunk Indian, for he proceeds to empty Deut's jug. Along the way, he engages in about the only ritual still meaningful in his life: "The Fish Hawk wasn't actually aware, any more, of who sat across from him in the dark; only a fellow drinker, from the long, half-forgotten line of fellow-drinkers. The jug passed in silence, the moon reflecting from its smooth sides" (70). By that method, deliverance from the present can be reached: "The whisky, because it dulled the senses and evoked long-forgotten emotions, let the mind of a man forget, then remember" (61).

It is in a state of lingering drunkenness that the Fish Hawk makes the blunder that costs his dog, Ebo, its life, when they come upon the bear early the next morning. Just as surely the Fish Hawk's life is forever changed: ". . . his whole body ached with weariness and a great revulsion for what he was" (88). Solemnly he carries the body of the dog into ". . . a great hollow where the huge white oaks stood like cathedral pillars in the silence of early morning" (92). There he buries the dog: "He was as gentle as a man covering a child with a blanket, and as quiet" (93). As he carefully completes the grave, the Indian undergoes a change: "Though the Fish Hawk never worried much about the significance of a spirit world, it came to him now, with moving poignancy, that he wanted very much to go wherever Ebo was going to be." To reach that goal, he makes two resolves, to quit drinking and to return to the White River country of his childhood. Without whiskey he will have to face the present, which means facing the future, which is death; when death comes, he wants to be worthy of it, thus he intends to cease being a "tame Indian" (131) and to return to the country and ways of his ancestors, there to await his call.

There is reason to delay his departure for a while, though. He has a hunch that Ebo has sired the pups that Sal, the Boggs hound, drops, and he wishes to honor the continuity of Ebo's life by rearing one of them. While he waits for the pup to be weaned, he participates in the process of continuation by passing on his knowledge to Corby. It is at this time that he teaches the boy the real meaning of killing a wild animal: it is not merely a ritual of skill and superiority, but a part of the natural order of things by which man promotes his own welfare (121–122). A process of equivalent importance is the gathering of remedy herbs, another gift of the forest (123). Accepting the end of his own life, the Fish Hawk finds satisfaction in thinking that his knowledge will survive him: "This fall, more than any of the others he had known, seemed to him to be the autumn of his life, and it was fitting, somehow, that he lend his knowledge and ability to the others who would live after him. It gave a deep satisfaction to be able to explain a fact of life to Corby, who was like a book of blank pages, waiting for someone to fill it with writing" (125). He realizes, too, that his action honors the past: "The things he had been able to teach the boy, the things he had done for Corby, were a last payment to the white man who had taken him as a boy and raised him long ago" (144).

During this time, too, even as he thinks of Corby's opening future, the Fish Hawk is reminded that participation in the ritual of closing is equally important. A wild boar has fatally injured Towsack Charlie, and the Fish Hawk, mindful of his promise, sees to it that Charlie is "doctored good and buried right" (43). He had not intended to return to the town, the site of his degradation, but his duty to Charlie demands it; he does indicate his new sense of purpose by refusing to sleep in the jail (181). That purpose is reflected in the assertiveness he displays in managing the funeral; he knows where to locate the money that Charlie had saved for just such a purpose, and he decides that Charlie's remaining bottles should be buried with him. There are others who disapprove of that gesture, but the Fish Hawk feels that Charlie ought to be able to take with him those things whose beauty gave him pleasure. At the same time, he is not unsympathetic to those actions considered ritually significant by others; when he is asked at the burial if he wishes to throw in the first shovel of dirt, he replies, "Don't reckon it makes a bit of difference, . . . but I will, if it's custom" (184).

Then the Fish Hawk returns to Boggs farm, to begin his hunt for the boar, which has proved itself a threat to human welfare. Patiently he tracks the boar until darkness, learning enough of the animal's habits to anticipate its behavior on the following day. As he makes his camp, he is joined by Corby, who still has the idea of killing uppermost in his mind; "I come to help you kill that boar" (193), he tells the Indian, and, later, when the Fish Hawk tells him to put his useless shotgun aside, Corby protests, "I want a chance to kill him" (194). When he is placated, Corby reduces his expectations slightly: ". . . I'll do it, whatever it is you want, . . . But I want to see him killed, if n I can't kill him myself" (195).

What the Fish Hawk wants is that Corby will allow himself to be stalked by the boar, while the Fish Hawk stalks the stalker. When the point is reached where the two hunters will separate, Corby has become sufficiently honest with himself that he does not need to assume a hunter's bravado. He can admit that he is afraid, trusting to the Indian's understanding: "'Me, too,' said the old man. He stuck out his brown hand and Corby shook it formally" (201). Rather than invoke a code of masculinity, or pat the boy on the head or shoulder to indicate his child's state, the Fish Hawk admits that it is not unmanly to be afraid, and shakes hands, as one man to another.

The hunting plan works. Despite his vigilance, Corby is surprised and terrified. But he is able to scuttle up a tree, as the Fish Hawk had directed him to do. There, understandably, he acts his age: he screams for the Fish Hawk. When the boy discovers that the Indian is present, he begs him to shoot, but the Indian has observed the boar long enough to detect something peculiar about it. To attract the boar's attention, the Fish Hawk speaks to it—in Osage. Thus he acknowledges the boar's connection with primeval times and his own similarity to the animal. For it is so old that it is nearly blind.

By tossing a stone or a stick or by calling to it, The Fish Hawk works the boar: ". . . the battle that followed was like a bullfight, . . ." (205). In a scene quite reminiscent of *The Sun Also Rises*, an intricate ritual which reveals the essential union of man's adaptability and nature's strength is played out. It easily assumes symbolic significance: the neophyte is clinging to the tree, the locus of wisdom, the Cosmic Pillar, in Mircea Eliade's phrase, as he observes the priest enact the right attitude toward the sacred, natural world.

Ten times the boar charges, then it just stands, grunting and gasping for air, waiting for the death that comes in nature when power is spent. The Fish Hawk tells Corby to descend: "We go"

(206). Still Corby is attached to the idea of the kill: "You ain't
going to kill him?" The Fish Hawk hands the rifle to the boy, but
the boy discovers that neither can he force himself to do it: "I
cain't, . . . I just cain't." And the priest recognizes a convert:
"The Fish Hawk placed his big hand on the boy's head."

Back at the farm, the Fish Hawk acknowledges that the ritual
was successful, that he has brought back a warrior from the
forest, by saying that Corby will relate the adventure. Then the
Fish Hawk feels that he is about to reach that state achieved by
his father: he believes that he will become a Little Old Man.
Among the Osages the Little Old Men were the older warriors
who had progressed from action to contemplation; theirs was the
possibility of observing the *Wah'Kon*, the Mystery Force,[3] as it
energized the countless forms of life, framing the rituals which
ordered their experience of those forms, and passing the
significance of the rituals on to the next generation. As Corby
begins, the Fish Hawk can take pride in success, for Corby
confesses that he had told a lie in order to join the Fish Hawk.
Then he tells his warrior's tale.

The Boggs men are incredulous. Grandfather Marcus is exas-
perated: "Well, I be goddam if I can understand a bit of it, . . .
You had him dead to rights and you never killed him" (212). The
Fish Hawk knows that he must sustain Corby: "The Indian
patted the boy's shoulder once, heavily." At the same time he
tries to convince Deut, the father: ". . . your boy, Deut, is
honest with himself. He has no need for the blood of a dyin'
animal to make himself strong, you see. He saw things the way
they was, and he let him go." Uncle Luke is hardly persuaded:
"I'd say any boy wouldn't know how to pull a trigger ain't hardly
a man" (213). The Fish Hawk cannot expect to save the entire
white race, so he rises to leave.

Down at the barn, Billy Firman proposes a farewell drink:
"Let's drink . . . to the old boar, and to the woods, and to ever'
thin' else that never will be seen again" (214). The Fish Hawk
sips and passes the cup to Corby, who manages to swallow without gagging. Then the two walk along, as Corby begs to go, even

in a woman's role: "I'll cook, or keep camp for you, . . ." With a smile, the Fish Hawk insists that Corby must remain, remain white: "From his pocket he took a necklace he had made from the teeth of the bear that had killed Ebo, and ceremonially he put it around Corby's neck." They reach the point where they must part; the Fish Hawk extends his hand, as to a man, but Corby cannot let it go. Gently, in recognition that a boy cannot become a man without some tears, the Fish Hawk withdraws his hand and pats Corby's head. "So long, Fish Hawk, . . . I'll remember you." These final words of Corby's are not designed to be sentimental—rather they complete the statement of the novel, for what is memory but the force which energizes the rituals that order our experience and give it significance, what are the rituals but the lessons that we have learned from our parents and that we must pass on to our children?

Thus the Fish Hawk steps out for the White River country, leaving behind no child but Corby. In concluding *The Last of the Mohicans* (1826), James Fenimore Cooper had the Indian sage, Tamenund, proclaim: "The pale faces are masters of the earth, and the time of the red men has not yet come again." Speaking from the time of the French and Indian War, barely into the red-white relationship, Tamenund envisions a time when the Indian could recover from his defeat. But even the prophet could not foresee genocide. Jayne's concluding sentence acknowledges that out on the dark fields of the republic such a thing occurred: "The Fish Hawk's blanket shone red, the barrel of the old Springfield glinted in a flash of sunlight, and then he was gone, into the woods that led to the White River, and the time that would never come again."

---

[1](New York: Pocket Books, 1970). Page references will be incorporated into the text.

[2]John Joseph Mathews, *The Osages: Children of the Middle Waters* (Norman: University of Oklahoma Press, 1961), 712, provides the citation of Cody's title.

[3]*Ibid.*, 20–30.

William Alexander Percy,
Walker Percy, and the Apocalypse

*I*n 1924 William Alexander Percy published his third volume of poetry, *Enzio's Kingdom and Other Poems*. The time for its writing had been snatched from a life that was otherwise given over to public demands. For Percy and his father, former Senator LeRoy Percy, were among those who had been occupied during the past several years in a furious battle to keep the Ku Klux Klan from establishing its control over Mississippi.[1]

Will Percy describes in his autobiography, *Lanterns on the Levee* (1941),[2] the onset of the Klan threat and the decision made by Greenville community leaders that LeRoy Percy should lead the defense, just as LeRoy's father had spoken for the town during Reconstruction times (*LL*, 274). Their community had not welcomed the original, postwar Klan, even though it had the Confederate cavalry tradition for cachet, and the new Klan was not about to be accepted. The Greenvilleans and others around the state were astonishingly successful in denying public acceptability to the Klan during those confused years, so that while the *New York Times* frequently detailed Klan activities in the South, and in the North (even on Long Island!), it remained silent about Mississippi.

Which is not to say that the Klan was totally frustrated in its Mississippi campaign. At first the citizens did rally to LeRoy Percy, who became a national anti-Klan leader. He spoke at rallies, some as far away as Chicago, and warned a national audience about "The Modern Ku Klux Klan" in the July 1922, *Atlantic Monthly*. His opponents were learning, though, to use the money they were accumulating through initiation and regalia fees and to use the advantages of secrecy and hierarchical organization. LeRoy Percy was forced to warn, in a letter to the

New York Times, on June 18, 1924, that the Mississippi delegation to the upcoming national Democratic convention had been
chosen by a Klan-dominated state convention. Some of the dele-
gates might not be Klan members, he acknowledged, but because of the unit rule the Klan would control the delegation.

The enemy may have been thrown off the walls and driven
through the skirts of Greenville, but the local victory was, to a
man of Will Percy's temperament, destined to be lost in the
general defeat. LeRoy himself might take comfort in a skirmish
worn—but Will was one to think always of the entire campaign.
The son could eat his greens only if they had vinegar on them;
commenting upon his father's success in winning a Senate seat,
Will observes, "Nothing is so sad as defeat, except victory" (*LL,*
145). Everything is sad, therefore, because nothing is absolute.

Even during the grand moments of '22 and '23, then, when
LeRoy was speaking, in Greenville, then elsewhere, Will would
have seen his father not as one man among a group of equal size
and density, striving toward some attainable goal, but as one
fully realized man against a background of smaller, insubstantial
figures, who were merely a part of "the sorrowful pageant of the
race" (*LL,* 234).[3] During those most rhetorical days, LeRoy became linked in Will's mind with Frederick II of Sicily (1194–
1250), the Sun King, the "Stupor Mundi"; for, as he wrote to
John Chapman,[4] he saw many a resemblance between his father
and the Emperor, whose presence he must have felt intensely
during his several visits to Sicily and Italy in the previous twenty
years. Dissatisfied with the unpoetic possibilities of his own
time, Will cast his father as Frederick II, in an extended narrative that ostensibly recounts Frederick's failure to attain his vision, but addresses as well his father's own inevitable failure.

The speaker of "Enzio's Kingdom"[5] is the thirty year old natural son of Frederick. King of Sardinia, Enzio had been his
father's first child, remained a favorite, developed into a de-
pendable and able military leader. But he had been captured by
the Bolognese, who refused to accept ransom for him, despite
Frederick's entreaties. He has languished a year in captivity,

therefore, despairing to hear of the disaffections among his father's followers, of illnesses that sap his father's strength, of unaccustomed defeats for his father's armies.

As the poem begins, Berard, Archbishop of Palermo, his father's oldest and most trusted friend, has entered Enzio's cell to tell him of his father's death. Enzio acknowledges the fatigue of his visitor, but wishes nevertheless to speak of his memories of his father. In Enzio's recollection, Frederick assumes a very specific character. Rather than possessing the outlook expected of a ruler of his time, he transcends history: Frederick's goal is not merely to increase his wealth or the size of his state, but to accomplish a grand design: ". . . after peace I shall enchant the world/Into a universal Sicily . . ." (CP, 311). He has in mind, in short, nothing less than the accomplishment of the millennium, that thousand years of peace prophesied in Revelations xx, the beginnings of which had been awaited in Europe since before 1000 A.D., when the expectation had become virtually universal.

Frederick is so captivated by the vision that he alone can realize that he prefaces a statement to his lieutenant, Pietro da Vigna, with an assurance: "When we have built the new Jerusalem . . ." (CP, 317). He alludes, of course, to that holy city which Revelations xxi prophesies will come down from God at the apocalypse. Frederick is mindful that he is claiming divinity for himself; in the same breath, he, like Jesus, puns upon the name of his chief subordinate, celebrating his rock-like role. The pun is not Percy's poetic fancy, but rather relies on history.[6] Both in history and in the poem, then, Frederick is to be perceived as a secular leader, who claims that his person, incarnating a divine presence, is to make a decisive, radical change in the unfolding history of the world.

With such a purpose, ". . . today in the great staggering world/ The only godlike, all-inclusive scheme/Of hope and betterment. . . ," Frederick feels justified in excluding himself from the laws which govern mere men: "Peace. Peace. The great prerequisite,/The race's single chance to reach its stature . . ./

There's not a lie too great, a crime too gross/I'll not be guilty of, if so thereby/I may establish it and fix the lines/Of the quivering vision I intend the world . . ." (*CP*, 311)

There is yet another likeness to Jesus which Frederick implies: just as He had chosen those who would be His intimate associates in spreading the Word, so does Frederick identify a "flashing-eyed minority,/The Enzios of the world, the sons of light" (*CP*, 312), to be turned "free-pinioned on an earth/That they would make august and radiant!" He will "concede the masses to the Pope:/Their stultified obedience makes for peace" (*CP*, 314). But he will not give his "eaglets to his cage:/For them there shall be freedom if it takes/The very toppling down of Peter's throne."

The freedom of which Frederick speaks is intellectual freedom: the inference to be drawn from all of his speech is that he intends to combat his enemies by making the truth established by empirical investigation the world's telling criterion. He therefore has already established his academy, in which the intellectual elite will be taught to govern with benevolence, within the limits of rationality and firmness: ". . . the young future teams/To Naples and Salerno where my schools/Are aids and urgers to the starrier way" (*CP*, 312–313).

History dictates the outcome of Percy's narrative. Frederick was excommunicated, anathematized, and deposed by the Council of Lyons, on July 17, 1235. All of Frederick's tributaries were freed of their allegiance to him, all legitimacy attached to his rule was denied. Percy pictures a scene in which Frederick attempts to combat the reawakened subservience of his followers to Papal domination by proclaiming the dawn of a revolutionary secular era. As Enzio recalls: "He dignified them with the truth," "As if they could partake of visioning" (*CP*, 327). But "they chilled: and slipped vague glances at their neighbors." Afterwards, Frederick tells Enzio what is inevitable: "The end. Darkness ahead. Darkness ahead" (*CP*, 329).

Like Jesus, Frederick is betrayed by his Petrus. Then, separated from his scattered sons, he dies a strangely muted death, of a broken heart, Enzio feels. In a sense, then, Frederick has given his life for his vision. Enzio will not allow himself to consider an alternative meaning: "I cannot see by what integrity/ High Heaven annihilated so his efforts!/Unless there be no heaven—and that I'll grant/Sooner than that his vision's fate was just! . . ." (CP, 341) Either an evil god or a godless universe— Enzio prefers the latter. If someday a divinity does appear, Enzio is confident that he will be "minded, willed, and souled" (CP, 342) like his father. Even though he will not be alive to see him, Enzio knows that in the coming of the avatar, Frederick will be resurrected.

In the Epilogue, Enzio reveals what has happened while he has talked through the night. In the short term, Enzio's senses have given him no information but the dispiriting; yet for the long term, now that he thinks about it, his intuition gives him a conviction of utter optimism—his father will return, someday, to fulfill his dream. So he concludes: "Some sky is in my breast where swings a hawk/Intemperate for immortalities/And unpersuaded by the show of death./I am content with that I cannot prove." (CP, 343)

Enzio thus convinces himself that his father had *really* defeated his two hateful enemies, the Papal institution, then still a major political force, and the Italian bourgeoisie, just beginning to realize its potential. Such seemingly unlikely allies were joined in the Guelph party; the merchants could lend great amounts of money at high interest to the Pope, who, not being threatened by their rise could bless their activity. The Emperor and his lords constituted the Ghibelline party; for all of his apparent openness to novelty Frederick actually represented the old order, which derived its wealth from land.[7]

Seeing Frederick II in these partisan terms enables us to understand why Will Percy really associates his father with Frederick. Senator Percy's enemies were the various groups— usually satirically portrayed by Will as eccentric mobs—that attacked the traditional Mississippi squirearchy. Certainly Will did not intend to suggest that his father made any kind of eschatological claims for himself or justified his own behavior by announcing himself an exception, but rather to celebrate his father as one of those leaders who are defeated in the ever recurring victory of darkness.

It is impossible to tell from "Enzio's Kingdom" what Will Percy may have known of the legends of Frederick that blew across Europe after his death. But even if they were totally unknown, those legends have a bearing here, insofar as they inform us of the tradition of Will Percy and help to explain why Walker Percy, Will's adopted son, has reacted so strongly and so repeatedly to his parent's code.[8]

After the death, in 1929, of LeRoy Pratt Percy, the father of Walker and his two brothers, Will Percy, LeRoy Pratt's cousin, invited the boys to live with him and, after the death of LeRoy Pratt's wife, adopted them. Thereafter, as Walker Percy has written,[9] Will Percy did not write much more poetry. No doubt he was too busy being a father—without the help of a wife or even the support of good health. He was a good father—we have Walker Percy's testimony to that. Indeed he was so conscientious a father that he struggled even in his poor health to pass on to his sons a sense of their tradition. Published in 1942, the year before his death, his memoir, *Lanterns on the Levee*, was dedicated to them. It is a thoughtful book. Every person of his tradition, Will Percy implies, has carried a lantern on the levee, helped in the communal effort to guard against the great external force which might at any time sweep away the results of man's work. The subtitle, "Recollections of a Planter's Son," grounds the tradition in local history.

Within the book, Will is at pains to spell out his views to his sons. Immediately he appears to be tracing his own life, but ultimately he is identifying those experiences which matter to him: his community, his family, his class, education, culture, activism. Very late he has a chapter, "For the Younger Generation," in which he distills his experience into a code for his sons: follow the ethics of Jesus and the stern inner summons of Marcus Aurelius. There are certain absolute values that are impervi-

ous to the pressures of irrational religion and base leveling.
"Love and compassion, beauty, and innocence will return. It is
better to have breathed them an instant than to have supported
inequity a millennium. Perhaps only flames can rouse man from
his apathy to his destiny" (*LL*, 313).

Having reached an apocalyptic climax in his peroration, Will
then lessens the tension of his argument, to talk first of the
failure of a philosophizing Christianity, which persists in its attempt to attribute divinity to Jesus, to promise eternal life, to
split hairs about the Godhead. Then he talks of the anesthetic
value to be derived from Aurelius' *Meditations*. From the two
models can be extracted man's limit/opportunity: to respect
himself, to respect others, to be open to the idea of a God—"it is
given to man to behold beauty and to worship nobility" (*LL*,
320). The best of all places to perform one's reverential gazing?
"I think if one would sit in the Greek theater above Taormina
with the wine-dark sea below and Aetna against the sunset, and
if there he would meditate on Jesus and the Emperor, he would
be assured a god had made earth and man." An allusion to Keats
completes the paragraph: "And this is all we need to know."

Yet despite the force and clarity of his Stoic message, Will
admits that many (and the implication is that some are nearby)
still trouble their hearts "with foolish doubts and unwise ques-
tionings—the fear of death, the hope of survival, forgiveness,
heaven, hell." He can only reply:

> Death, Heaven or Hell, Rewards or Punishments, Extinction or
> Survival, these are epic troubles for the epic Mind. Our cares are
> fitted to our powers. Our concern is here, and with the day so
> overcast and short, there's quite enough to do.
> So I counsel the poor children. But I look for the seer or saint who
> sees what I surmise—and he will come, even if he must walk
> through ruins. (*LL*, 321)

And so we are back to that yearning for the apocalypse that lurks
beneath the apparent iron control of the immanentist.

The legend of Frederick II, the tradition in which that legend
stands as a principal beginning, and the influence of that tradi-

tion upon modern political movements have been of particular interest since World War II. For there has been a rather wide recognition that the roots of Nazism lay in the tradition of which I speak, so that a tracing of the history of the tradition might account for the incredible ferocity with which adherents accepted Hitler *and* remained faithful to him to the bitter end. Still, though, one might object that Nazism is worthy of historical interest, no doubt, but of no more urgency than many another topic. On the contrary, as the analysts of the tradition point out, the same basic set of ideas that underlay Nazism provides the motive force for Marxism. When we read Eric Voegelin's *The New Science of Politics* (1952), or Norman Cohn's *The Pursuit of the Millennium* (1961), or Marjorie Reeves's *The Influence of Prophecy in the Later Middle Ages* (1969), then, we are struck not by the dated, "historical" nature of the reality being described, but rather by the frightening ease with which we can use descriptions of "medieval fanaticism" to deepen our understanding of today's headlines.

I refer specifically to the historical process which Voegelin describes as the redivinization of modern political mass movements.[10] Historians are agreed that the idea owes its basic stimulus to Joachim of Flora (1145–1202).[11] About 1190 Joachim, an Italian abbot, after years of isolated Scriptural study, conceived an idea whose time had come. While Scripture had always been interpreted for edifying purposes, Joachim discerned meanings that commented upon the current world situation and even forecast the plan according to which the future would be unfolded. His vision in all its intricacy Joachim called the "everlasting gospel," *evangelium aeternum,* in reference to Revelations XIV, 6. Fundamental to his scheme was the division of history into three stages, each presided over by a Person of the Trinity. The Father inspired the time of the Old Testament; the Son, the New Testament; and the Spirit would inhabit the millennium.[12]

By Joachim's calculations the third stage would begin sometime between 1200 and 1260. During the immediately preceding transitional period, certain actions must occur. There must be a new religious order to preach the new gospel; from this new order of spiritual men would emerge twelve patriarchs who would convert the Jews and a *novus dux* who would inspire the world to turn from materialistic to spiritual considerations. Exactly three and one half years before the fulfillment of the third dispensation, the Antichrist, the Last World Emperor, would destroy the corrupt and worldly Church, which presumed to place itself between man and God. Then with the destruction of the Church and the overthrow of the Antichrist, the millennium would commence.

Even at the moment of his birth, Frederick II was the object of eschatological expectation, for there already was a legend of the Emperor who would preside over the Last Days. As he matured, he and his lieutenants apparently believed in his divine destiny. Needless to say, the Pope and his party were of a different mind. Thus Frederick developed two legendary personalities, exactly opposed. To his German supporters he was to be the Emperor who would usher out the last secular age by conquering the real Antichrist, the Pope, then become the *novus dux* who would usher in the new world in which his lieutenant, Pietro da Vigna, would be the new Pope, his earthly representative. The new world would be free of institutions (and their attendant quarrels) because all activity would be subsumed to *one* institution. To his Italian opponents, he was the Beast of the Apocalypse who must be fought not merely as a secular, but as a demonic, threat, with every resource available. Frederick, in short, sets in the European imagination the legend of the secular leader who comes in the fullness of a known scheme; who commands absolute obedience; who in order to fulfill his destiny must purge his people of their traditional institutions (so that his personality, the only institution, will expand to its possibility and) so that they can respond to the truths of their blood; who will lead them to victory if they are worthy or to destruction (the very fact of which would be proof that they had not risen to his visionary demands).

If the figure of Frederick was not stripped of its eschatological promise by his death, neither was Joachitic thought discredited by the eventual decline of the Frederick myth. On the contrary, the basic features of the Joachitic scheme have continued to assert themselves in European political philosophies for seven hundred years. Eric Voegelin was particularly interested in the phenomenon, for he saw it as the modern manifestation of gnosticism, a religious stance that has always appealed to those weak in the faith. Disagreeing with those who had argued that modern political mass movements were neopagan, he countered that such movements, because of Joachim, actually represented a rejoining of the secular and sacred streams of history that St. Augustine had separated. Such movements as Nazism and Marxism and such philosophies of history as those of Condorcet, Turgot, Comte, Hegel, and Marx reflect, therefore, a vision in which God (especially the Redemptive Christ) has been replaced by History.[13] These various visions are generally agreed upon their "aggregate of symbols which govern the self-interpretation of modern political society": (1) the sequence of three ages; (2) the exalted leader; (3) the prophet of the new age (who is sometimes also the leader); and (4) the brotherhood of autonomous persons, who are the apparat of the prophet and the leader.[14]

All four of Voegelin's case symbols are to be observed in "Enzio's Kingdom." Most are directly stated: it is laboring the obvious to remind the reader that Frederick is an autocrat (2), that he as leader has himself for ideologue (3), that he employs his sons (and by extension all those bright young technocrats in his schools are his "sons") to vanquish the old so as to realize the new (4). Only the three-ages concept (1) must be inferred, but there are several data to support that inference. There is, for one thing, Frederick's repeated reference to the nearness of the millennium. Corollary to his belief in the millennium is his rejection of Christianity: ". . . I see the thing that calls itself/Christ's Church a noble detriment, a dream/Once valid, but in the dawning old and evil" (*CP*, 314). Percy imputes to Frederick a belief in the "hidden god" known to the gnostics[15]: "Three is enough: yet not enough, I know. . . ./Jesus, Mahomet, Abraham—good men/Guessing! I read their words with reverence/ And know that still the ultimate word's not written . . ." (*CP*, 314).

Granted, Frederick did not destroy the Church or achieve the millennium—in his *first* life. But he will return, in the "guise" of others, "minded, willed, and souled like him." There is also the implied sequence of time-spirits in the poem: Frederick himself was born into the Age of the Father, in which fear and servitude have dominated the experience of life; Enzio represents the Age of the Son—his attitude toward his father reveals his faith and filial submission. Frederick had hoped to lead his youth, "the sons of light," in the Third Age, the Age of the Spirit, in which he "would change all this: and for imperial boon/Grant freedom to the spirits of the free" (*CP*, 312). Although the age of the Spirit has not been reached, at the end of the poem, yet it is ever about to be reached, for at any time, Enzio feels, a return of Frederick's spirit may occur.

Will Percy's apocalyptic imagination is further revealed in *Lanterns on the Levee*. The most striking evidence of it is the arrangement of three scenes that conveys Will's conception of history as a sequence of ages. First in the series is the description of Will's grandfather, "Fafar," who had led the community during the reestablishment of white supremacy. He had been so sure of the rightness of his view that he had broken mere laws to accomplish it. Percy's father, LeRoy, "considered Fafar superior to any human being he had ever known: he insisted he had a finer mind, a greater gusto, a warmer love of people, and a more rigid standard of justice than any of his sons" (*LL*, 274). Second in the series Will Percy describes LeRoy's leadership of the community in repelling the invasion of the Klan (*LL*, 225–251). LeRoy's conduct in the Klan episode was without reproach, was representative of his life: small wonder that Will worshipped him as LeRoy worshipped "Fafar." Those men, the fathers, belong, in Will's mind, "on the west portal of Chartres with those strong ancients, severe and formidable and full of grace, who guard the holy entrance" (*LL*, 74). The third scene—in which Will Percy was called upon in 1927 to lead the community through the crisis of the great Mississippi flood—marks the decline. Honest enough to describe himself as having done a creditable job, Will nevertheless has to distinguish his behavior from that of his legendary fathers. Like Enzio at the knee of Frederick, Will had listened to his father (*LL*, 75), but somehow the moves that he made did not fully accomplish the wisdom that he had heard. He includes in the story an account of his having made what in retrospect he sees as a mistake and his father's having perpetrated a gentle subterfuge in order to allow him to save face. Will feels compelled, too, to admit that he became so exhausted that he had to resign his position, to go to Japan for a vacation. Further, he must say that "the two really great contributions made to the Delta by the Red Cross had been made without me and without my connivance" (*LL*, 269). There is, then, a tendency to see a radical hiatus between his fathers and himself, even as he tended to see each crisis in his own life not as an opening toward possibility, but a continued drift toward chaos.

The Age of the Son will not be a time of joy or victory. Writing in 1941, Will Percy sees Frederick's scorned "masses" everywhere triumphant: "in Russia, Germany, and Italy Demos, having slain its aristocrats and intellectuals [read "fathers"] and realizing its own incompetence to guide or protect itself, . . . submitted to tyrants" (*LL*, 312), while in the Western democracies Demos had grown bloated and corrupt. "We of my generation have lost one line of fortifications after another, the old South, the old ideals, the old strengths" (*LL*, 313): the end of the age is bound, undoubtedly, to be destruction.

Which will, of course, to a practiced apocalyptist, be man's salvation: "Perhaps only flames can rouse man from his apathy to his destiny" (*LL*, 313). But how can man be prepared to fulfill his destiny? The failed son must pass on to his sons the tradition of the fathers and the advice that his sons can only endure stoically until the new age commences: "So I counsel the poor children. But I long for the seer or saint who sees what I surmise—and he will come, even if he must walk through ruins" (*LL*, 321). Thus William Alexander Percy left a legacy that one son, Walker, has described as Southern Stoicism.[16]

Walker Percy's first novel, *The Moviegoer* (1961),[17] is dedicated "in gratitude to W. A. P." It would have looked, then, to anyone who knew of the relationship between the two men that Walker was emulating the behavior of his adoptive father. And it could have been assumed that the content of the book would be inspired by the older Percy's code. A reading would have confirmed that assumption, for there is a character, Aunt Emily, who is clearly modeled after Uncle Will, who walks, like Uncle Will and his Stoic models, as she ponders the decline of the old tradition.

The relationship of the statement of *The Moviegoer* with the code of Will Percy, though, is not finally a comparison, but a contrast. To be sure, there have been readers who have dismissed the protagonist as merely a weak, feckless young man of the modern persuasion and who have thought that Aunt Emily was intended to speak the author's piece in her great broadsword-swinging speech toward the end of the novel (*M*, 219–227). But the statement of the novel, less eloquent, less obvious, is that one must reject the grimly satisfying pessimism about the present, the reveries about a legendary past, and the utterly baseless hankering after a post-apocalyptic paradise (*M*, 231). The old tradition must, in other words, be rejected. It can be respected as a good-faith effort in its time, but its present use would be indefensible. In that first novel Walker Percy is quite restrained in describing its baneful effects upon his protagonist (perhaps because of his recognition of its value in its original context), and even after the old code is rejected, the protagonist remains on good terms with its spokesman, Aunt Emily, in fact stands in her good graces, so that the unwary reader might be tempted to think that Binx Bolling has finally come to his senses and accepted the rightness of his aunt's code.

Walker Percy is not so temperate in his second novel, *The Last Gentleman* (1966).[18] The protagonist, Will Barrett, suffers from several disabilities, both physical and mental, that derive from his complicated linkage to the past. The novel traces his return to the South, even as he seeks deeper within himself to discover the cause of his distress. Thus he comes finally to his hometown, to approach the domain of his father by way of the levee:

> Here he used to walk with his father and speak of the galaxies and of the expanding universe and take pleasure in the insignificance of man in the great lonely universe. His father would recite "Dover Beach," setting his jaw askew and wagging his head like F. D. R.:
>
> > *for the world which seems*
> > *To lie before us like a land of dreams,*
> > *So various, so beautiful, so new,*
> > *Hath really neither joy, nor love, nor light,*
> > *Nor certitude, nor peace, nor help for pain—*
>
> or else speak of the grandfather and the days of great deeds . . . (*LG*, 309–310)

Then Will approaches the house, to recall those dangerous times when his father had confronted and defeated a Klan-like organization. He remembers the night when the police came to tell his father that the intruders had left: ". . . there was a dread about this night, the night of victory. (Victory is the saddest thing of all, said the father)" (*LG*, 331). He had pleaded for his father not to leave him, but the father had gone upstairs and killed himself. For, according to the logic of the apocalyptist, if there is to be no apocalypse, then suicide is the only deliverance from everydayness. In *The Moviegoer* Percy had not openly asserted the eventual self-destructiveness of the apocalyptist; he had used only a shadowy father, who had grandly volunteered to fight in World War II, succeeding "not only in dying but in dying in Crete in the wine dark sea" (*M*, 157). His death, if not by his own hand, was nevertheless a suicide. In *The Last Gentleman* Percy does not dodge: separated from the legendary assurance of the fathers, the father turns ironic enough to kill himself and leave a horrified son. But Will must reject the stance of the lost son: he may grieve over his father's decision, but he does not have to honor it. The father was wrong, simply wrong. Freed of the ghost by even breathing such an antipatriarchical idea, Will is ready to go forth to build his own life.

Tom More, in the third novel, *Love in the Ruins* (1971),[19] sees himself precisely as Uncle Will's "seer or saint" who will walk through the ruins.[20] His mind is dominated by the gnostic tendency to devise schemes of time. He breaks the continuity of American history into century-chunks, for example. The year is 1983, hard upon the *annus apocalypsis* prophesied by George Orwell. From the present he works backward, to 1883, to 1783, to 1683, to . . . Eden (*LR*, 57). Destroyed by the white man's mistreatment of the black man and the red man, the American Eden can be restored—if Tom More uses his miracle, the lapsometer, the last word in technology. It will thus be the American spirit which becomes the Third Rome and brings universal peace. Whoever really believed the eschatological myth of Russia as the Third Rome? "And as for Russia and the Russian Christ who was going to save Europe from itself: ha ha" (*LR*, 58).[21] On the contrary, it will be a Louisiana Christ; appropriately, Tom More ignores the religious significance of Christmas Eve in order to gloat over his scientific breakthrough.

There is yet another scheme of time: while Tom does not acknowledge it, he must, as an American and a Southerner, recognize the significance of the first four days in July. In the first age, 1776, those days marked the completion and announcement of the American testament, the Declaration of Independence; surely 1776 was the time of the fathers, the Founding Fathers. In the second age, 1863, the defeat at Gettysburg and the surrender of Vicksburg on July 4 determined the ultimate destruction of the South; this must certainly be the age of the sons, as Lincoln recognized in "The Gettysburg Address." But even though the Union endured, the rending of the American fabric occurred, so that by 1983 every aspect of American life is polarized. Only Tom More has the technology, that body of knowledge that constitutes immanent man's chief glory, to resolve the tensions and usher in the millennium—or, if the apocalypse occurs, lead the survivors into a new Eden, such as is prefigured by the Honey Island experiment.

Except that—Tom More causes mischief rather than good. His machine, that is to say, all technology, further alienates by exaggerating, rather than diminishing the fragmentation of the human community. His Faustian dream is burlesqued by the appearance of a wacky Mephistopheles. The idea that Tom could cure the world when he cannot even cure himself! He had hoped to supplant his symbolic father: whereas Saint Thomas More had only planned a Utopia, Tom had visions of using the old American know-how (and Japanese sub-contractors) to make it. Rather he must call on Saint Thomas to protect him; he still needs a father, after all. And in the Epilogue, he has a father, Father Smith. It is Christmas Eve and time for confession. Tom has been chastened from secular time schemes back to the Christmas event, the Incarnation. The novel is truly a comedy, in that all is concluded in a state of bliss; but the great fun provided by Walker Percy's glorious imagination should not cause us to forget his deadly serious theme, that modern man is ever a prey to his own gnostic longings.

It is soon apparent in Percy's fourth novel, *Lancelot* (1977),[22] that he is still concerned with the fatal ease with which the Southern ideal becomes a gnostic nightmare. In ordinary time the year is 1976; for the protagonist it is one year after the apocalypse. For Lance Lamar had literally walked through the ruins the previous year; at that time he had revealed the bitchery of his wife (and therefore all women), had executed her lover (and in the doing killed three other people, his wife included), and had experienced the explosion of his ancestral home. Miraculously uninjured, he had walked into the charred ruins to retrieve his weapon, a Bowie knife, which to him symbolizes the "broadsword tradition" which had inspired his past behavior and also the "sharp twoedged sword" of Revelations with which he will accomplish his future project. Even though he is at present confined to a "Center for Aberrant Behavior."

The initial situation of the novel thus bears an uncanny resemblance to that of "Enzio's Kingdom." The protagonist is a captive, who begins to spin out for a visitor an account of the events that led to his being where he is. There is one significant difference between Enzio and Lancelot, though: whereas Enzio is submissive to his fate, understands that he will die a prisoner, can only await the father-like seer who will come (return), Lancelot, convinced that his survival is a genuine miracle, must be thereby assured that he is destined to be the seer.

As he begins to talk to his silent visitor (like Berard a priest) Father John, an intimate friend from childhood, Lancelot describes his life in the years that they have been separated.[23] He had grown up in the Southern tradition, had excelled as an extrovert, had married his virgin, Lucy. He had, in other words, thrived in an immanent world, while maintaining what his tradition identified as the romantic ideal.

Then Lucy died, wasted away, as illusions do. Lance had lived on at Belle Isle with his mother, becoming more and more of a drunken recluse, marking time as a small town lawyer with a light caseload. When he met Margot Reilly, costumed as a Southern belle, but soon revealed as a wanton Texan, Lance thinks that he can have it both ways. As his wife, she can provide the cold cash to restore his estate and the warm flesh to reawaken his manhood.

The marriage eventually lapses into habit, though; Margot restores the house and becomes bored; Lance no longer finds her novel and is bored. She becomes restive, and he lapses back into his everydayness, drunkenness, TV watching, and ever more frequent occasions of impotence. In time he discovers her infidelity. It should be clear that the severity of Lance's response to Margot's behavior is not just caused by his sense of betrayal by or jealousy of another human being. He never makes a single effort to speak to Margot—rather he reacts with such cold, obsessive fury because he had cast a role for her in his personal allegory. Her defection announces her escape from his mind into autonomy, tears apart his absolutist distinctions between ideal and real. Thus he feels that the apocalypse must come: all is darkness, evil, filth, bitchery, buggery, betrayal.

Lance systematically sets out to create the "flames." There is natural gas seeping to the surface in the cellar of his house; Lance plans to use it to create his ball of fire. So he pipes it into the ventilation system; then, armed with that legendary weapon, the Bowie knife, he goes forth to wreak vengeance, an insane man acting with monstrous cruelty in emulation of the legendary decisiveness associated with his patriarchical ancestors.

The novel is a brilliant, bitter comment upon the danger of acting in response to the appeal of a mythic past. For the past, as we retrieve it, undergoes simplification, fabrication, distortion: but even if we could know it in all its complexity, we would still be grotesque fools to imitate a past action, for that action was appropriate only to its own context. But there is more: the mythic past serves in the novel as the ground out of which a malicious vision of the future can grow. After all, millennial blueprints turn out to be the architect's conception of lost Eden.

Lance is so emboldened by his successful action, by which he has leaped the actuality of his father—a provincial poetaster, who conspired in his own betrayal—to behave with all the righteous force of his ideal father, that is, the legendary father, that he now intends to apply his purging wrath to the entire country. He *knows* now that the Third Age is beginning. The First Age lasted from 1776 to 1861, the Second Age from 1861 to 1976 (*L*, 157); the Fathers conceived of a grand idea, the Sons allowed it to perish in materialism. Did not his own father accept a bribe? Would one of his patriarchs have done that?

It will be up to Lance, then, to publicize his full understanding of the coming age. And so he gradually, over the several days that he speaks to Father John, amplifies his daydreams into a vision into a philosophy. And himself to act upon his knowledge. He recognizes the dread dissociation of sensibility in the modern world, knowledge severed from will. But he, acting both as seer and as leader, possesses "both the conviction and the freedom" to "start a new order of things" (*L*, 156), to be accomplished by his brotherhood of autonomous persons. Walker Percy has thus consciously satisfied Voegelin's criteria for gnostic self-representation in his creation of the character of Lancelot.[24]

Lancelot, then, is among other things a total rejection of "Enzio's Kingdom." William Alexander Percy had asserted that it is noble to dream of a millennial state which would be the restitution of the mythic world of the fathers. Walker Percy, no doubt with sadness, must counter that it is ultimately insane to dream of an immanent millennial state, for the dream sooner or later entices the dreamer to think of himself as God. Our sense of alienation is the only proof that we need to convince us that we are not God. Thus we *must* experience the loss of the father, then go forward in faith, toward the only paradise, our communion with the transcendent Father.

The loss of the father is precisely the theme that haunts Percy's latest novel, *The Second Coming* (1980).[25] It turns out that Will Barrett (of *The Last Gentleman*) had soon concluded that Sutter Vaught, the alienated physician, was an unfit father-figure. Thus he had returned from the apocalyptic Southwest to settle down in the secular city. There in New York he prospered as a lawyer and husband to a wealthy woman. Almost before he knew it, she had died and he had retired to the southern mountains—the Sewanee locale always recalls lost Eden in Percy's work.

There he plays golf, in Percy a game that both exercises and apotheosizes. Except that he has been beset by falling; it is no wonder that he has developed a bad slice. And at the same time he has begun to be bothered once more by the mystery of why his father had tried to kill him and why he had, on a second attempt, killed himself. As befits a self-conscious Hamlet, Will keeps a toy of desperation in his glove compartment.

If his life had remained perfect, he probably would have killed himself. His present bores, and his past either cannot be faced (his father's ghost) or cannot be retrieved (the highschool cheerleader whom only now he has begun to remember). But then his condition deteriorates to the point that he wanders off the fair-way, leaves the right of way, crosses a zone.

In an abandoned greenhouse, Will meets Allie Huger, who should be named "Grace"—*alleluia!* She, it turns out, is Kitty Vaught's daughter: Will is to have a second chance at life, a second coming into the world. In midlife, then, flagging Will is to be lifted by Allie, who is a "hoister." Not that Will has sense enough simply to accept his good fortune; who among God's stubborn children does? Deciding to put God to the test, Will hides himself in a cave, to see if He will come after him (for all the "adult" seriousness about the gamble, there is a certain lu-dentic air about it, as when a child hides in the closet—to be found, for otherwise the game is no fun). But nothing more numinous than a toothache nudges him out of the cave—not into a contemplation of Plato's distant Sun, but plop into the greenhouse, born again.

There Allie cares for him and accepts his love, becoming that miracle who both mothers and mates. Together they share a consciousness and build a world, get as close to Heaven as it is possible in North Carolina. Then Will can finally throw those haunted weapons into the abyss, transcend the susceptibility to depression he has in his blood. Lifting up his eyes to the hills, he organizes a group of rest home relics as a construction company. Although he found love in the ruins, he now wants to build anew, as a man will when he has faith in the future. There will be no apocalypse, but rather the second coming that has oc-curred for Will and Allie, now sexual and spiritual, but prefiguring a Communion that transcends even those ecstasies.

---

[1] Richard H. King, "Mourning and Melancholia: Will Percy and the Southern Tradi-tion," *Virginia Quarterly Review,* 53 (Spring 1977): 248–264, explores Will Percy's rela-tionship with the tradition of the fathers. He does not deal, though, with Will Percy's inclination toward the apocalypse or with Walker Percy's response to his adoptive father.

[2] William Alexander Percy, *Lanterns on the Levee* (Baton Rouge: Louisiana State University Press, 1973), 225–241. Hereafter, references are included in the text as *LL*.

[3] The last paragraph of *LL* confirms Will Percy's conception of history as frieze: "Here among the graves in the twilight I see one thing only, but I see that thing clear. I see the long wall of a rampart sombre with sunset, a dusty road at its base. On the tower of the

rampart stand the glorious high gods, Death and the rest, insolent and watching. Below on the road stream the tribes of men, tired, bent, hurt, and stumbling, and each man alone. As one comes beneath the tower, the High God descends and faces the wayfarer. He speaks three slow words: 'Who are you?' The pilgrim I know should be able to straighten his shoulders, to stand his tallest, and to answer defiantly: 'I am your son.' (*LL*, 348)

[4] Phinizy Spalding, "A Stoic Trend in William Alexander Percy's Thought," *Georgia Review*, 12 (Fall 1958): 248.

[5] The text of the poem herein used is in *The Collected Poems of William Alexander Percy*, forword by Roark Bradford (New York: Alfred A. Knopf, 1943). Hereafter, references are included in the text as *CP*.

[6] See Ernst H. Kantorowicz, *Frederick the Second, 1194–1250* (New York: Frederick Ungar Publishing Company, 1957), 511–513.

[7] Thomas Caldecot Chubb, *Dante and his World* (Boston: Little, Brown and Company, 1966), 105–112.

[8] In "Walker Percy's Southern Stoic," *Southern Literary Journal*, 3 (Fall 1970): 5–31, I explore Walker Percy's reaction in his first two novels to Will Percy's Stoicism. In "*The Moviegoer* and the Stoic Heritage," in *The Stoic Strain in American Literature*, ed. Duane J. MacMillan (Toronto: University of Toronto Press, 1979), 179–191, I trace the Stoic tradition in Southern history in a very cursory way.

[9] Walker Percy provides an "Introduction," vii–xviii, to the LSU Press reprint of *LL* being cited in this paper.

[10] Eric Voegelin, *The New Science of Politics* (Chicago: The University of Chicago Press, 1952), 107.

[11] Majorie Reeves, *The Influence of Prophecy in the Later Middle Ages* (Oxford: Clarendon Press, 1969) is a full-length treatment of Joachim.

[12] Norman R. C. Cohn, *The Pursuit of the Millennium* (New York: Harper and Row, 1961), 99–123.

[13] Voegelin, 111–112.

[14] Voegelin, 112.

[15] See discussions of the "hidden god" in Hans Jonas, *The Gnostic Religion* (Boston: Beacon Press, 1958), 42–43, and in Robert McQueen Grant, *Gnosticism and Early Christianity* (New York: Columbia University Press, 1966), 97–119.

[16] Walker Percy, "Stocism in the South," *Commonweal*, 64 (6 July 1956):342–344.

[17] Walker Percy, *The Moviegoer* (New York: Noonday Press, 1967). Hereafter references to *The Moviegoer* are included in the text as *M*.

[18] Walker Percy, *The Last Gentleman* (New York: Farrar, Straus and Giroux, 1966). Hereafter references to *The Last Gentleman* are included in the text as *LG*.

[19] Walker Percy, *Love in the Ruins* (New York: Farrar, Straus and Giroux, 1971). Hereafter references to *Love in the Ruins* are included in the text as *LR*.

[20] In his early essay "The Man on the Train" (1956) Percy discusses the alienated man's hankering after "the old authentic thrill of the Bomb and the Coming of the Last Days. Like Ortega's romantic, the heart's desire of the alienated man is to see vines sprouting through the masonry." "The Man on the Train" is included in *The Message in the Bottle* (New York: Farrar, Straus and Giroux, 1975), and is the text herein cited, 84. Also "Notes for a Novel about the End of the World," obviously an essay bearing upon the apocalypse, is included in Percy's collection of essays.

[21] Voegelin, 114–115, discusses the tradition of Russia as the Third Rome.

[22] Walker Percy, *Lancelot* (New York: Farrar, Straus and Giroux, 1977). Hereafter references to *Lancelot* are included in the text as *L*.

[23] I speak to Lance Lamar's Southern background in "The Fall of the House of Lamar,"

in *The Art of Walker Percy: Stratagems for Being,* ed. Panthea R. Broughton (Baton Rouge: Louisiana State University Press, 1979), 219–244.

[24] Cleanth Brooks, "Walker Percy and Modern Gnosticism," *Southern Review,* 13 (Autumn 1977): 677, receives credit for first remarking upon similarities between Eric Voegelin and Walker Percy. In "The Gnostic Vision in *Lancelot,*" *Renascence,* 32 (Autumn 1979): 52–64, I cite Percy's specific reference to *The New Science of Politics* and describe the way in which Percy uses Voegelin's analysis of modern gnosticism to create a psychology for Lance Lamar.

[25] (New York: Farrar, Straus and Giroux, 1980).

APPENDIX

Soon after the War, the *New York Times* (11/11/66), adolescent but already assuming to speak for the nation, editorialized about the Southern novel. It began with that soft voice of happy disappointment common to editorial writers and schoolmarms: "We had thought that the war, and the political results which have followed the war, had put an end to the habit which was so common before it, of obtaining sectional patronage for books, and other articles of merchandise, by designating them as 'Southern.'" Such a habit, the editorial very patiently explained, "can only do damage in destroying the feeling of *Americanism* and *nationality* which ought to be impressed on the juvenile mind." "But," the *Times* continued, "we see that the mania for dubbing all such things, and many other things, 'Southern,' where they are intended for a Southern market is again abroad among Northern manufacturers."

The editorial did not offer an example of a Southern novel. Nor did it offer a test for detecting one, such as newspapers used to provide for counterfeit banknotes. It did not require a certain quality or level of intention. It did not specify that it was speaking of novels written by native Southerners, or of novels with Southern settings, or of novels seriously dealing with a "Southern" theme, or of any combination of the above. It simply assumed the validity of its generalization and an audience which would accept that generalization.

The following list rests on the same assumptions. There was a Southern novel, and the War did not kill it. *Selah!* There was a Southern novel, and the *New York Times* could not kill it. *Selah!* There is still a Southern novel, over a hundred years later, even in a South that has become, says Walker Percy, "happy, victorious, Christian, rich, patriotic and Republican." *Selah!*

Southerners who published first novels between 1940 and 1983 include:

Virginia Abaunza	Paul Allan
Warren Adler	Sarah S. Allen
James Agee	William Allen

Lisa Alther
Barbara Anderson
Elizabeth Andrews
Ramon Andrews
Raymond Andrews
Maya Angelou
Evelyn Anthony
Harvey Aronson
James Aswell
Philip Atlee
Margaret Atwood
Barbara Averitt
Charles Baker
Gladys Baker
James Ballard
Toni Cade Bambara
Margaret Culkin Banning
Jay Barbee
Jane Barry
John Barth
Richard Bausch
Gordon Baxter
Ann Beattie
Robert Bell
Vereen Bell
Peggy Bennett
Wendell Berry
Doris Betts
Louise Blackwell
Marcus Boggs
Paul Darcy Boles
Leigh Borden
Edgar Bowers
Blanche McCrary Boyd
Taylor Branch
Matthew Braun
Joanna Brent
Christopher Brookhouse
Joe David Brown

Rita Mae Brown
Frederick Bueckner
Jackson Burgess
Bettz Burr
Carl Burton
Octavia E. Butler
Jack Cady
Will D. Campbell
William T. Campbell
Vincent Canby
Robert Canzoneri
Truman Capote
Clancy Carlile
Jess Carr
Hodding Carter
Rebecca Caudill
W. W. Chamberlain
Jerome Charyn
Thomas Chastain
Alice Childress
Billy C. Clark
Frank Clarvoe
John Bell Clayton
Walter Clemons
Patricia Cloud
Carlyn Coffin
Virginia Coffman
Elizabeth Boatright Coker
Lonnie Coleman
William Laurence Coleman
Alice B. Colver
James Conaway
Caroline B. Cooney
Pat Conroy
R. C. Cook
John William Corrington
Kathleen Crawford
Hubert Creekmore
Harry Crews

John Crosby
Louise Crump
Dick Dabney
Lucy Daniels
Guy Davenport
Muriel Davidson
Anne Mallard Davis
Burke Davis
M. H. Davis
Paxton Davis
Robert P. Davis
Wesley Ford Davis
Babs Deal
Borden Deal
William Demby
Maurice Denuzere
James Dickey
Georgia di Donato
Ellen Douglas
Harris Downey
Allen Drury
Andre Dubus
Julia Coley Duncan
Wilma Dykeman
John Ehle
Julie Ellis
Garnett Epps
John Farris
John Faulkner
John R. Feegel
Peter Feibleman
Alice Fellows
Chris Ferguson
Jeff Fields
Foster Fitzgibbons
Fannie Flagg
Jack Flam
Inglis Fletcher
Candace Flynt

Shelby Foote
Jesse Hill Ford
Richard Ford
Robert H. Fowler
William Price Fox
Ernest Frankel
Ben Friedman
Charles Gaines
Ernest J. Gaines
Frances Gaither
David Galloway
George Garrett
Zena Garrett
John Garth
Chloe Gartner
Patricia Geary
Ben Geer
Peter Gent
Robert Gibbons
Jewel Gibson
Barry Gifford
Ellen Gilchrist
Barbara Giles
Henry Giles
Frankcina Glass
Gail Godwin
Laurence Gonzales
Stephen Goodwin
Arthur Gordon
Christine Govan
William Goyen
Alice Wentworth Graham
Shirley Ann Grau
Pat Graversen
Edith Pinero Green
Lewis W. Green
John Howard Griffin
Leon Griffith
Ken Grimwood

Winston Groom
Nicholas Guild
Peter Guralnick
Frances Gwaltney
Elizabeth F. Hailey
Linda Haldeman
B. C. Hall
Earl Hamner
Barry Hannah
Alberta Pierson Hannum
Elizabeth Hardwick
Stephen Harrigan
Evans Harrington
William Harrington
Charlain Harris
William Harrison
Scott Hart
Mildred Haun
Laurie Havron
William C. Haygood
Joseph Hayes
Shelby Hearn
William Heath
Ann Hebson
Worth Tuttle Heddon
Paul Hemphill
Helen Henslee
Robert Herring
John Hewlett
Jean Heyn
Daniel Hickey
Don Higgins
Pati Hill
Tom Hillstrom
Richard Himmel
Burt Hirschfeld
James E. Hitt
Michael P. Hodel
Jane Aiken Hodge

William Hoffman
Mary H. Hollingsworth
Henry Hornsby
Katherine Hoskin
May D. Hoss
Edwin Huddleston
Tom E. Huff
William Bradford Huie
William Humphrey
Mary Fassett Hunt
Evan Hunter
Mary Vann Hunter
Mac Hyman
Bowen Ingram
Caroline Ivey
Quida Jackson
Randall Jarrell
Mitchell Jayne
Gregory Jaynes
Charles Johnson
Charlotte J. Johnson
Ellen T. Johnston
Victor Johnston
Carter Brooke Jones
Douglas C. Jones
Madison Jones
Donald Justice
John Katzenbach
Terry Kay
Norman Keifetz
Douglas Kiker
Joseph O. Killen
John D. Killens
Edward Kimbrough
Chuck Kinder
Florence King
Edythe Kirkland
Richard Kluger
John Knowles

Avery Kolb
Elizabeth Kytle
Speed Lamkin
Bob Lancaster
Dorothy Langley
Edythe Latham
Leroy Leatherman
C. P. Lee
Edna Lee
Harper Lee
Joshua Lee
Christopher T. Leland
Warren Leslie
Edward Levy
Mark Lieberman
Romulus Linney
Norris Lloyd
Betsy Lochridge
Margaret Long
Roger Longrigg
Walter B. Lowrey
Beverly Lowry
John Lutz
Herbert Lyons
Thomas McAfee
Cormac McCarthy
Jame McIlvanie McClary
Carson McCullers
John P. McDonald
James Lee McDonough
Edwin McDowell
Bruce McGinnis
Amanda Mackay
Eric Mackensie-Lamb
James McLendon
Bonner McMillion
Larry McMurtry
James Alan McPherson
David Madden

Gary de Maria
Robert Marks
Robert K. Marshall
Valerie Martin
Bobbie Ann Mason
Graham Masterton
Alfred Maunde
Hamilton Maule
Gilbert Maxwell
Julian Mayfield
May Mellinger
Richard C. Meredith
Robert B. Merkin
Barbara Michaels
Heather Miller
Vassar Miller
Charles Mills
Lionel Mitchell
Robert Molloy
Marion Montgomery
Bucklin Moon
Barbara Moore
Berry Morgan
Willie Morris
Suzanne Morris
David Morton
Jane Morton
Albert Murray
C. S. Murray
Robert Louis Nathan
Gloria Naylor
Gay Weeks Neale
H. L. Newbold
David M. Newell
James R. Nichols
Nancy Nichols
Christina Nicholson
Helen Norris
Hoke Norris

Flannery O'Connor
Charles O'Neal
George Patterson
Richard North Patterson
Frances Patton
Edwin Peebles
Walker Percy
Elizabeth Peters
Brenda Peterson
Robert Deane Pharr
Thomas Hal Phillips
Ovid Williams Pierce
Josephine Pinckney
Clark Porteous
Charles Portis
C. E. Poverman
Crawford Power
Eugenia Price
Reynolds Price
Clay Putnam
Lloyd Pye
Dotson Rader
Robert Ramsey
Mark Raney
Julian Lee Rayford
Bryon Herbert Reece
Ishmael Reed
Jessie Rehder
Anne Rice
Judith Richards
Robert Richards
Pierson Ricks
Alexdra Ripley
Harold Robbins
Lettie Rogers
John B. Rosenman
Fred Ross
Louis D. Rubin, Jr.
Virginia L. Rudder

Jane Gilmore Rushing
William Russell
John Fergus Ryan
J. R. Salamanca
Ferrol Sams
Thomas Sancton
George Scarborough
Alison Scott
Glenn Scott
Philip Scruggs
Chris Segura
Mary Lee Settle
Michael Shaara
Doris Shannon
James Sherburne
Louise Shivers
David Shobin
Celestine Sibley
Susan Sibley
Anne Rivers Siddons
Andrew Sinclair
Verna Mae Slone
Dave Smith
Lee Smith
Lillian Smith
Pat Smith
Patrick D. Smith
William Ferguson Smith
Ellease Southerland
Terry Southern
Elizabeth Spencer
Anne Nall Stallworth
Dorothy Standfill
Max Steele
Martha Stephens
R. T. Stevens
Barbara and Dwight Stewart
John Craigh Stewart
Ramona Stewart

James Still
Hart Stilwell
Elna Stone
Philip Stone
James Street
Walter Sturdivant
Edward Swift
William Styron
Walter Sullivan
Hollis Summers
Cid Ricketts Sumner
Robert Tallant
Peter Taylor
Leslie Thomas
Michael Thomas
Carlyle Tillery
B. S. Tillinghast
John Kennedy Toole
Jane Trahey
Lael Tucker
Anne Tyler
Helen Upshaw
Alice Walker
Margaret Walker
Leslie Waller
John Evangelist Walsh
Eugene Walter
Evelyn K. Ward
Lella Warren
Sterling Watson
Gordon Weaver
John D. Weaver
Robert Weekley
Gus Weill
Linda Weintraub
John L. Weldon

Manly Wade Wellman
Eudora Welty
David Westheimer
Elizabeth Wheaton
Guy Wheeler
James Whitehead
Phyllis Whitney
Tom Wicker
Allen Wier
Robert Wilder
John Hazard Wildman
Sylvia Wilkinson
Gordon Williams
Joan Williams
John A. Williams
Tennessee Williams
Vinnie Williams
Wirt Williams
Calder Willingham
John W. Wilson
Donald Windham
William Wingate
Anne Goodwin Winslow
Leonard Wise
Burton Wohl
Miles Wolff
Charles Barnette Wood
Stuart Woods
Bronté Woodward
Sean M. Wright
Wyatt Wyatt
Vurrell Yentzen
Jefferson Young
John Yount
Lee Zacharias
N. Zaroulis

INDEX

Adams, E. C. L.: his *Congaree Sketches* and *Nigger to Nigger,* 20n
Agrarianism: Fugitive concept of, 12
Allen, James Lane, 4
American Mercury, 11
Anthony, Legend of St., 34–35
Antoninus, Marcus Aurelius: his *Meditations,* 128
Arnold, Matthew: his "Dover Beach," 135
Arnow, Harriette: her *The Dollmaker,* 18–19
Augustine, St., 35
Awful, the Sense of the: Tennessee Williams's justification for the use of the grotesque, 18

Baldwin, Joseph G., 15
Barnes, Carmen: her *School Girl,* 8
Barnes, Hazel E., 56n
Basso, Hamilton, 6; his *Relics and Angels, A View from Pompey's Head,* and *The Light Infantry Ball,* 9
Befindlichkeit, Heidegger's concept of, 99
Bethea, Jack: his *Cotton,* 20n
Bible, as source of imagery, 60, 61, 63, 73, 74; Genesis, 70; Job, 69, 72, 74; Ecclesiastes, 16; Matthew, 25, 26; Mark, 27; Luke, 74n; John, 26, 27; Romans, 46; Revelation, 124, 129
Bookman, The, 10
Boyd, James: his *Marching On,* 20n
Bradbury, John M.: his *Renaissance in the South* acknowledged, 20n
Bradford, Roark: his edition *The Collected Poems of William Alexander Percy,* 142n
Brickell, Herschel: his "The Literary Awakening in the South," 10
Brooks, Cleanth: his "Walker Percy and Modern Gnosticism," 143n
Broughton, Panthea R.: her edition *The Art of Walker Percy: Stratagems for Being,* 143n
Bunting, Charles T.: his "An Afternoon with Walker Percy," 107n
Byrd, Scott: his "Mysteries and Movies," 106n

Cabell, James Branch: 3, 6, 7, 9; his *The Way of Ecben,* 8
Cable, George Washington, 4, 15
Caldwell, Erskine: his *The Bastard,* 8; his *God's Little Acre,* 9
Calvin, John, 24
Camus, Albert: his *The Stranger* as source for Richard Wright's *The Outsider,* 38; likeness of Cross Damon to Meursault, 53
Capote, Truman: his *Other Voices, Other Rooms,* 18
Carr, John: his "Rotation and Repetition: Walker Percy," 107n
Cash, W. J.: his "The Mind of the South," 11; his *The Mind of the South,* 20n
Caste in American literature: dark man as teacher of white boy, 109

153